PROFANE
EVANGELISM

ALSO BY MARK E. VAN HOUTEN . . .

God's Inner-City Address

PROFANE EVANGELISM

Taking the Gospel Into the "Unholy Places"

MARK VAN HOUTEN

Ministry Resources Library

Zondervan Publishing House • Grand Rapids, MI

PROFANE EVANGELISM
Copyright © 1989 by Mark E. Van Houten

Ministry Resources Library is an imprint of Zondervan Publishing House, 1415 Lake Drive, S.E., Grand Rapids, Michigan 49506.

Library of Congress Cataloging in Publication Data

Van Houten, Mark E.
   Profane Evangelism : taking the Gospel into "unholy places" / Mark E. Van Houten.
      p.   cm.
   ISBN 0-310-51951-9
   1. City churches. 2. Evangelistic work. 3. Van Houten, Mark E. I. Title.
BV637.V37   1989   89-36762
269'.2—dc20   CIP

Whenever possible, non-gender-specific pronouns have been used in this book when gender is irrelevant or when the reference includes both men and women.

All Scripture quotations, unless otherwise noted, are taken from THE HOLY BIBLE: NEW INTERNATIONAL VERSION (North American Edition), copyright © 1973, 1978, 1984 by the International Bible Society. Used by permission of Zondervan Bible Publishers.

Edited by Lori J. Walburg and Michael G. Smith
Designed by James E. Ruark

Printed in the United States of America

89 90 91 92 93 94 95 / PP / 10 9 8 7 6 5 4 3 2 1

To Paul and Margaret, Dad and Mom,
primary mentors in evangelism
for ten children to the glory of God.

All the names of the people and most of the place names in this book have been changed to respect the confidentiality requested, assumed, or expected by these people and around these places.

In addition, I have chosen at times to record the actual speech of my parishioners, even when such speech may be crude or offensive. My intent in recording such language is not to shock or offend, but to offer a more accurate picture of inner-city ministry.

Contents

²profane *adj* [ME *prophane,* fr. MF, fr. L *profanus,* fr. *pro-* before + *fanum* temple — more at PRO-, FEAST] (15c) . . . **profaneness** *n*

—Webster's Ninth New Collegiate Dictionary

Preface

If, on some corner of two streets in some neighborhood, I were to place a large bucket upside-down and stand right next to it six hours a day, four days a week, nearly everyone in the neighborhood would begin speculating as to what is under that bucket. Many people would ask others their opinions and some would undoubtedly declare with utter confidence exactly what was underneath. And those who believed "the experts" would go and tell others what they were told.

Since no one would actually have seen what was under that bucket, questions would remain in nearly everyone's mind. Some people would be fearful. They would surmise that since the world is so full of evil, there must be some sort of evil under the bucket.

Someday, however, it is likely that someone would muster the courage to look under the bucket. And when others saw that the person who looked under it was unharmed, they too would investigate. As people finally realized that what was there is for the good of all the people, the bucket would then no longer be feared, but valued, treasured, protected, and celebrated.

In Uptown, the Chicago neighborhood to which I am called

to minister, I see myself as that bucket. For six hours a night, four nights a week, I am involved in evangelistic work. My approach is analogous to the upside-down bucket. Nearly everyone knows about buckets and their purpose, yet if one is seen in an unconventional place, it becomes a curiosity. Nearly everyone knows about Christians and their purpose. But if one is seen in an unconventional place, it is a matter of curiosity.

This curiosity factor is what makes evangelism work for me. Evangelism is simply Christians making known that God is the Master and Savior of all and that he is immanent and concerned with the lives of those who bear his image. The reason the curiosity factor is effective in evangelism is that the recipients of the Good News themselves discover what God wants them to know rather than have it pushed on them.

What is it about a Christian's presence in some communities that makes him or her a curiosity? It is that the Christian is obviously "out of place" or "in the wrong place." People expect to see Christians in churches, in suburban shopping malls, in "wholesome settings." But when Christians are in "unholy places," they are a curiosity.

When Christians appear in profane places, they draw attention to themselves. Christians are not generally known for their profaneness. To be profane literally means to be "before [that is, outside of] the temple." When Christians are willing to exhibit profaneness—that is, when Christians effectively demonstrate that neither they nor the God whom they profess is restricted to a temple that is generally open one out of seven days a week—then non-Christians will be interested in understanding more.

Christians who are willing to spend time outside the temple arouse interest in God and in Christian living. To exercise profaneness is to testify concerning God as he really is; namely, God is everywhere relevant and relevant everywhere. People become disciples; they accept God's lordship and commit themselves to him because another Christian has entered into the world to demonstrate God's grace, not in spite of that act. That is the thesis of this book: Christians are able to evangelize most biblically and effectively as they incarnate Christ and exhibit and exercise the best of the Good News about God; that is, when their presentation of God is not anchored in the ontological, but in the functional attributes of God.

You have heard that it is said, "You are the salt of the earth." I tell you the truth, your salt will remain in storage unless you become a valued, treasured, protected, and celebrated bucket in your community.

Mark Van Houten
Passiontide 1988
Chicago

Part One

EXPLAINING PROFANE EVANGELISM: The Sound of One Hand Clapping

"But Nineveh has more than a hundred and twenty thousand people who cannot tell their right hand from their left, and many cattle as well. Should I not be concerned about that great city?"

—Jonah 4:11

Chapter 1

On the Road to Emmaus

More than three years have passed since I first introduced myself to the Chicago neighborhood of Uptown, where I am currently fulfilling my commission to inner-city ministry. I will never forget that first day in Uptown. Before I abandoned the safety of my car for a more intense, personal visit, I drove around at length to get a feel for the community, to obtain a sense of this neighborhood's pulse, breathing, disposition, and temperament.

On this atypically hot and humid May day, I saw faces in which were lodged hollow and hopeless eyes. These faces, bruised, scratched, stitched, disfigured, downcast—really, *de*-faced —belong to women and children as well as to men and boys. The smell of urine stung my nostrils, and the stench of vomit nauseated my stomach. Both sight and smell testified that the people of this community were the dispossessed. Like sheep without a shepherd, they were the harassed and the helpless.

On foot, I explored Wilson Street first. It seemed to be the inheritrix of the most blighted people and places in Uptown. As I was walking by the Indian Trail Saloon I saw an old black man bending forward at his waist, his torso parallel with the ground. Elbows locked and hands nearly swiping the ground, this man, Jamul, was holding one aluminum can in each hand. Chanting fiercely, Jamul raised first one arm, then the other, then swung his hands together full force, banging the cans. He did this methodically, again and again, his chanting so loud that it almost drowned out the clashing of the two cans.

In an attempt to get by Jamul unnoticed, I snuck around his backside, hugging the wall of the Indian Trail Saloon. I was immediately behind Jamul when he suddenly stood upright, turned to face me, and forced his spiral eyes to focus in my direction. Then without warning, he took a swipe at the side of my head with one of the cans, now dangerously jagged-edge and sharp from his ritual. I managed to block Jamul's shot, and he danced away laughing hysterically.

My first thought was, "Lord, have mercy [on me]." My second thought was, "Lord, where are you in all of this?"

A Faulty Theology

Unlike the gentlemen with whom Jesus walked on the road to Emmaus, it took me eight months, as opposed to half a day, to see that Jesus was at my side and at the side of the residents of Uptown. *Like* the gentlemen with whom Jesus walked on the road to Emmaus, my perception was myopic because I had forgotten some basic teachings that are woven into and emphasized throughout the Scriptures. The single most important teaching that I had forgotten is that God is ubiquitous.

Certainly God is with his church. But there are also places where God is where the church is not. In fact, God is everywhere that the church is not. Our Lord does say that "where two or three come together in my name, there am I with them." He did *not* say, however, that where there are *not* two or three gathered in his name, he will *not* be there also.

I can scarcely believe the subtlety and cunning of Satan. What an ingenious trap he had devised! I had fallen into a snare perfectly suited to a person of middle-to-upper-class status: the trap of arrogance. I believed wrongly that God somehow depended on me for access to Uptown. With typical upper-class pride I acted like a privileged landholder of private property, property that no one, including God, could enter without my blessing.

How could I have possibly thought that God needed me to introduce him into Uptown? He was there all along. Once he opened my eyes, I could no longer help but see him everywhere. But I had been blinded to God's presence by a faulty theology that misinterpreted Scripture. Just as Jews have been blinded to the fact that Jesus of Nazareth is the promised Messiah, so I was blind to the presence of God in Uptown.

Acts 28:23–31 is a classic summary of why Jews were blinded to the presence of God in his Son. Like me, they worked with a faulty theology, but theirs was one that mistook the purpose of the Messiah. To understand the similarities between the two faulty theologies, we need to look in depth at the passage in Acts 28.

[The Jews] arranged to meet Paul on a certain day, and came in even larger numbers to the place where he was staying. From morning till evening he explained and declared to them the kingdom of God and tried to convince them about Jesus from the Law of Moses and from the Prophets. Some were convinced by what he said, but others would not believe. They disagreed among themselves and began to leave after Paul had made this final statement: "The Holy Spirit spoke the truth to your forefathers when he said through Isaiah the prophet:

" 'Go to this people and say,
"You will be ever hearing but never understanding;
    you will be ever seeing but never perceiving."
For this people's heart has become [fattened];
    they hardly hear with their ears,
    and they have closed their eyes.
Otherwise they might see with their eyes,
    hear with their ears,

> understand with their hearts
> and turn, and I would heal them.'

"Therefore I want you to know that God's salvation has been sent to the Gentiles, and they will listen!"

For two whole years Paul stayed there in his own rented house and welcomed all who came to see him. Boldly and without hindrance he preached the kingdom of God and taught about the Lord Jesus Christ.

Rabbi Halter Speaks

Consider with me what a Jew of Paul's day might have thought about the apostle and his message.

It was 4:30 on a hot summer afternoon. I was walking briskly through the marketplace on the east side of Rome, a turban wrapped around my face to deaden the stench of livestock and rotting vegetables. Around me, vendors shook their fists and shouted, as much threatening their buyers as luring them to their wares. Everywhere children, animals, and men jostled for space, and I danced from one shifting spot of space to another, dodging merchants' tables, vendors' carts, and various four-footed beasts.

I was heading for the northeastern most of the seven hills of Rome, my nightly venture after a hectic day of lecturing at the synagogue. There I had found a lonely outcropping of rock where I could meditate and pray. There a cool breeze washed over me, and I would watch the rocks color, then darken, with the setting sun. Thinking of my destination as I pushed my way through the crowd, I was surprised to hear my name being called.

"Rabbi Halter! Rabbi Halter!" shouted one of my students, pushing his way through a group of women. I stopped and waited for him to catch up to me, his face earnest and sweaty. "The Sanhedrin is about to meet in an emergency session, and they sent me to find you."

I glared at him impatiently. "What is this 'emergency'?" I snapped. "Couldn't it wait until tomorrow's session?"

The young man, sensing my impatience, explained quickly. "Paul of Tarsus has just arrived in Rome, and the council is meeting to arrange a time to talk with him."

My irritation vanished immediately upon hearing the student's words. For some time now I had wanted to hear more about this new sect that Paul represented. "You lead the way," I ordered the young man, and we hurried back through the crowded marketplace.

In council with the Sanhedrin, we arranged to meet Paul on a certain day. Since he was bound while awaiting trial and not free to come to the synagogue, we went to him. I think half of the Jews in Rome came to hear Paul on that day. From morning till evening he explained the kingdom of God and tried to convince us that Jesus was the Messiah predicted by the Law of Moses and the Prophets.

Some of the Jews were convinced by what Paul said. Whether or not they actually became Christians, I do not know. Most of us Jews would not believe. Most of us got caught up in our own little arguments which, I must admit, were actually peripheral to that about which Paul was testifying. We began to leave. Before we were able to leave, however, Paul made one final statement. He said that the Holy Spirit had spoken the truth to our forefathers through the prophet Isaiah.

Isaiah had told our forefathers that, no matter how much they heard or saw, they would never understand or perceive because their heart had become fattened, their ears hardened, and their eyes closed. Isaiah went on to say that if our forefathers' hearts had not become fattened, they would have been able to see and hear with their eyes and ears, understand with their hearts, and turn back to God, who would heal them.

Now, I can understand why God gave this message to Isaiah to deliver to our forefathers. The Jews of Isaiah's day were a self-centered people. They thought they were such special people that no matter what they did, God would be on their side. Even after God banished them to exile, our forefathers nurtured the fantasy that they were somehow God's last great hope. They did not see that God intended to work his way and his will through them; rather, they thought that they *were* God's way and God's will.

Why Paul felt that these words from the prophet Isaiah were
equally applicable to us Roman Jews, I will never quite understand.
After all, we do not think that we are the answer to God's promises.
We realize that we must look for a Savior out of the line of David
who will establish the kingdom of God among us. This new king of
ours will be the most wise and powerful king this earth has yet seen.
He will reclaim our native land and reestablish us Israelites to our
proper place as rulers of this earth under God.

I think all the confusion rests with Paul. After all, he spends an
inordinate amount of time talking about that man Jesus. Yes, that is
where his confusion must lie. How could Paul possibly believe that
that Jesus fellow is the Messiah promised in the Old Testament
Scriptures? Jesus was a nobody, a poor preaching rebel, an insecure,
demented man. How could Paul, with all his education, possibly
believe Jesus to be the Messiah, especially after he died without so
much as a whimper!

Yes, that is where I am butting heads with Paul—over that
man Jesus. For Jesus was not the Messiah; I will guarantee you that.
The ancient Scriptures point to a Savior who will rescue and redeem
his people Israel and restore us to our proper place. Jesus was no
Savior, but a weak and pitiful man, and I have no desire to hear
more from Paul or anyone else about this bogus "Messiah."

The Apostle Paul Speaks

Now consider with me what Paul's thoughts might have been
after this particular interaction with the Jews.

Ever since Christ called me to apostleship and evangelism, I
had been determined to get to Rome to preach the kingdom of God
and Christ crucified. Well, I have been here in Rome for two weeks
now, and I have to tell you, they have been two of the most
disappointing and difficult weeks in my life. The last two weeks
make the treacherous, year-long voyage to get here seem like a
dream vacation.

For starters, I was informed upon my arrival that I have to
remain bound by chains to a Roman soldier at all times until my

trial takes place and I am either acquitted or imprisoned. On top of that, here I am, not only living in the country, but living in the *capital city* of the country of which I am a native-born citizen; where I am treated like a common criminal—guilty before proven innocent! My trial is not even scheduled to take place for another whole year.

Even worse, I have not been allowed the freedom to enter into the Jewish synagogues and preach, which is what I came here for. If I had known this was going to happen, I would never have appealed to Caesar in the first place. . . . Well, maybe I would have. God has worked out his way and his will despite the circumstances.

I think Anatolus, the Roman soldier to whom I am bound by chains, has become a Christian through all this. And I have been allowed a house as opposed to a cell. Consequently, enough Jews have come around that I was able to have them convince the Sanhedrin to set up a meeting between myself and what must have been close to half the Jews in Rome. A Rabbi Halter was particularly instrumental in setting up this meeting.

Still, just when I thought things were starting to improve, the meeting itself was a disaster. For a whole day I explained to them the kingdom of God and tried to convince them about Jesus from the Law and the Prophets. Very few were convinced, and I doubt whether any of them actually came to a saving faith in Jesus Christ. At day's end, most of the Jews were arguing amongst themselves about everything but Jesus. They were wholly unresponsive to the possibility of Jesus' being the Messiah.

As you know, in every village, town, or city I have ever entered, I have always gone first to my fellow Jews. They were God's only choice for spreading the news of his plan of salvation before Christ actually came. It seemed only right that they be given the first opportunity to declare the coming of God's kingdom to the Gentiles. However, few Jews have believed in Christ, and even fewer have acted upon this calling and privileged opportunity.

Let me tell you why this is so. The pre-Messianic Jews had their own great commission of sorts. The Scriptures illustrate a nation of people who, out of sheer grace, God chose to be his instrument of proclamation and witness to all the nations concerning the Hope-to-come; that is, concerning Jesus, who now has come.

Of course, the Israelites were not expected to send out apostles and evangelists. Rarely will an Israelite go to other nations to bring news of God. The prophet Jonah was one such exception. By and large, however, the Israelites were to proclaim the Messiah-to-come by being a model nation with God's help. Do you remember, for example, all those Mosaic laws concerning the *goyim*, the foreigners? God demanded an extra measure of love and justice from the Israelites toward the foreigners. Why? Because he wanted the Israelites to pull the foreigners, as it were, into a relationship with himself, complete with hope in the Savior-to-come.

In other words, the great commission of the pre-Messianic Jews involved a pulling-in, an attracting, or *centripetal* mission. The nation of Israel was to live in such a way that all other nations would be attracted to its axis, which was none other than Jehovah God.

The Jews prior to Christ had a very basic problem with self-centeredness. Again and again God sent prophets to shake them out of their selfishness. The Jews never listened, however, and in their self-centeredness they failed in their fundamental calling and purpose. The pre-Messianic Jews failed in their centripetal mission.

I really thought things would be different after Jesus our Savior had come. I really thought the Jewish people would see the light. Christ has come and has given the Jews a second chance and a new commission: they are again called to bear witness. Now, instead of *goyim*, we call the foreigners Ethnics or Gentiles. Instead of witnessing to the Hope-to-come, the Jews are to witness specifically about Jesus Christ, the Hope who *has* come. And instead of a centripetal mission plan, God has called the Jews to a *centrifugal* mission plan.

The Jews are to *go out* to the other nations and declare the coming of the kingdom in our Lord Jesus Christ. Needless to say, the Jews still cannot hear the Word of God. Isaiah's words are still relevant because the Jews continue to be self-centered, blind, and deaf. Because they want a Savior on their own terms, the Jews fail to see that Jesus of Nazareth is the promised Savior. They fail to see this despite the fact that he fulfilled all the prophecies. For the same reason that the Jews under the Old Covenant failed in their centripetal mission, the New Covenant Jews deny their centrifugal mission.

The good news is that after the Jews left, God allowed me to stay in my own rented house, and I welcomed all who came to see me. I preached the kingdom of God boldly, and without hindrance I taught about the Lord Jesus Christ. In other words, against all odds, God enabled me to carry on! Against all odds, salvation has been sent to the Gentiles, and the Gentiles are listening!

Working Outside the Temple

Christians in twentieth-century America unfortunately may exhibit the same attitudes as Jews in first-century Rome. Thinking of themselves as God's chosen people, they erect temples where they can meet, set apart from the rest of the community. They return to the old centripetal model, hoping that the easy witness of a building may pull outsiders into their inner circle. Instead of going out, these Christians sit inside their temples and await the second coming of their powerful, judgmental Messiah. Or if they do go out, they drag behind them the ball and chain of their holy temples.

To truly fulfill the centrifugal nature of the Great Commission, Christians must go *out* into the world and leave the confines of their "holy temples" to take the gospel into profane places.

Evangelistic efforts will not be successful if we confine God to our temples theologically and practically. God is both inside and outside of our churches—whether we define church as brick and mortar or as flesh and blood. Jesus did not establish an earthly kingdom confined to certain people in certain places and certain times. No. "The earth is the Lord's and the fullness thereof."

In many ways God is more like the world outside our brick-and-mortar churches. The people outside our churches are highly mobile. Already in the Old Testament Jehovah revealed himself as a mobile God, preferring a portable sanctuary to a permanent temple. While other gods required submission only while one remained on their turf, Jehovah went with the Israelites into exile, and it was on "another's" turf that he showed himself to be the Lord of history and time.

Our God is not a "Home Sweet Home" God. Precisely because he is a nomadic and nonspatial God, it was in exile that the Israelites came closest to fulfilling the will of God. Jesus continued this tradition. He did not leave a handbook on the church as an organization; he left a community. Jesus discouraged his disciples from building a permanent structure at the place of Transfiguration. The destruction of the temple as Jesus so often predicted is a very profound statement on ecclesiology. The earliest disciples not only understood but clearly exemplified this nomadic character, since they were known as "the People of the Way" even before they were known as Christians.

None of this is to say that there is anything wrong with flesh-and-blood temples seeking a meaningful relationship with God in a brick-and-mortar temple. My primary contention is that in order for Christians to be effective evangelists, they must acknowledge that God is not bound by either of these types of temples. If, with Saint Paul, we acknowledge that God will work his way and his will in history with or without us, then it will be helpful in terms of evangelism to leave ourselves open to the possibility that perhaps God has gone before us with his Good News.

In other words, rather than requiring or expecting a community to respond to the church, a church must respond to the community. The church must identify and join in the work God is already doing in the world. God is ubiquitous. God precedes us to the mission field. Unless our eyes are opened to this fact, we will be as hopeless and helpless as the two with whom Jesus walked on the road to Emmaus. Christians cannot evangelize relevantly in a dynamic and rapidly changing world with a static theology. We often speak of evangelizing people no matter who they are. It is more helpful to speak of evangelizing people no matter *where* they are.

A directly related principle of evangelism is that if the church is to become known, it must first come to know. It must seek out the lost, often going into profane places to do so. That is what I discovered after another visit to the Paper Nickel Bar.

As I entered the bar I saw Prieta in tears for what seemed to be the hundredth time in two years. The reason for her tears was virtually always the same. I saw that this instance was no exception as she uncovered her blackened right eye. Her husband had beaten her again.

Prieta had trusted me only about half the time over the past two years. Tonight she decided to trust me with her grief and her problems again. "Mark," she sobbed, "may I have a shoulder to cry on?"

She was sitting in a booth, across the table from someone who had been trying to help her—someone whom I had seen maybe two dozen times previously, but who had never said a word to me. After I listened to yet another episode of horror between Prieta and her husband, this man finally spoke to me.

"I must confess," he began, "even though I've seen you in this bar and in this neighborhood a lot, I never talked to you because I thought you were a fraud. I couldn't believe that a true minister of God could come into a bar. I imagined all sorts of horrible reasons why you might impersonate a minister. I thought you were a fake. Now I've seen you help Prieta and know that I was wrong—that you must be a great friend. Please forgive me."

Must the church become known or come to know? Many church people are smugly wrapped up in the belief that the *goyim* see their place of worship, see them enter and exit worship once or twice on the Sabbath, and therefore know all that they need to know about the church but simply refuse to be a part of it. But have you ever wondered what the neighborhood people think a churchgoer does besides entering and exiting a church? Do you think they have any conception of your life and work outside the holy temple?

In truth, the neighborhood probably thinks of churchgoers in terms analogous to a light switch: "It's Sunday, let's turn the light on, for we have lived as we pleased and have sinned on Monday through Saturday." Such a thought is too often perfectly consonant with the way we live the rest of our lives in North America. Got a headache? Pop a pill. Spouse no longer feed or fertilize your ego? Get a divorce. Facing your emotions too painful? Get drunk. Reality too unrelentingly brutal? Watch television. Feel guilty? Go to church.

The church must become known. But the full answer to my question, "Must the church become known or come to know?" is that we must both become known and come to know, and we cannot become better known unless we better come to know. Not only did this middle-aged man not believe that I could possibly be a minister in a bar, but he was scared to death of the prospect that I could be a faithful, committed, and sincere minister and be in a bar. Otherwise he might have to accept God on God's terms and according to God's schedule rather than merely when God was most convenient to him.

A Place for Jamul

Jamul is mentally ill. He is one of many mentally ill who roam Uptown since the emphasis on deinstitutionalization began in the mid-seventies. Word has it that Jamul became mentally ill when crooked accountants and lawyers wrested from Jamul's ownership a few million dollars' worth in property titles. Now Jamul has nowhere to go and nothing to do. He is always pleasant and agreeable in demeanor, but when he has been drinking, his play— although he is not aware of it—can be dangerous, both to himself and to others. At times Jamul runs around like a madman and pays no attention to traffic. And sometimes, hitting in fun, he strikes someone who does not know him, and that person, thinking Jamul is out to hurt him, sometimes lashes back.

When Jamul is drunk, he almost always regresses mentally to a time when he was six years old. Often he will lie on his back on the sidewalk next to a metal pole, banging out a tune on that pole with a rock or a stick or whatever he finds handy, and sing in a cheerful but awful voice. Once while he was sober, Jamul told me that this banging and singing is a song that he sang at age six when, for disobeying, he was sent to bed without supper and sang himself to sleep. (Come to think of it, Jamul always does end up sleeping where he does his clattering.)

Jamul is aware of the fact that he can choose what community to hang out in. So why does he continue to hang out in Uptown? The answer is profound. Where else in society can Jamul be where people do not mind entertaining him when he acts like a six-year-old? Where else in our society would people make sure that Jamul will not cross the street when he might be struck by a car? Where else in our society will people make sure that strangers who misunderstand Jamul's play will not hurt him? Where else can Jamul go and be joyfully entertained, cared for, and given respect and dignity? The answer is that God placed Jamul in Uptown and was with him even before a Christian befriended him.

Chapter 2

On the Road to Damascus

My parents are beautiful and powerful Christians. They are also committed Christians who never gave a second thought to the tremendous sacrifices they made in order to give each of their ten children twelve years of costly Christian education. I was packed with Christian head-knowledge at an early age. Also at an early age—eight years old to be exact—I first noticed the Holy Spirit intensely at work within me to make this head-knowledge become heart-knowledge. About a year later I took this head-knowledge to heart. No one could ever convince me at that time, or since, that there is not a God who by his grace has saved me and all those who will simply believe on his name and accept his Son's gift of eternal life.

God also told me—by the simple method of dropping the idea into my thinking—that he had a special purpose for my life. He told me that I was going to serve him in some kind of direct way. At the time, I was hearing a lot of missionary tales, and because I was an adventurous young person, the danger and challenge of mission life fascinated me. So right away I took God's general message to mean that I was to become an overseas missionary.

Between the sixth and seventh grades I began to tune God out, and for about a year I had no idea what I was going to do with my life. Even though I was young, I worried about the future. I could have avoided this if I had just put my trust in God and continued to heed the Holy Spirit's leading. Instead of trying to figure out what *I* was going to do with my life, I should have been asking God what *he* wanted to do with my life.

In the seventh grade, while I was grieving the Holy Spirit by shutting my ears to his plan for my life, he confronted me once again with the idea of ministry. A teacher who was impressed with my God-given insight into biblical matters said several times during the year that I should seriously think about going into the ministry. I tried to give this teacher the impression that I would never even bother to consider such a suggestion. (It was not "cool" in seventh grade to want to be a preacher.) I continued toward Damascus.

In my freshman year of high school I was sure that I would have an outdoor job. I was going to enjoy life working with my hands, working hard and to the best of my ability. But once again I was not allowing the Holy Spirit to work in my heart for guidance, so he used physical means to guide me. My feet were bothering me, and I went to a podiatrist. After examining me, the doctor said that if I tried to make a living doing manual labor I would not last five years. He advised me to get a good education because I would be best off with a white-collar job. The Holy Spirit could not have told me in a more concrete way that I was to go to college. He led me to see that I had to go to college even though I was trying to block out his voice in this part of my life.

Still I clung to my egotistical nature and refused to listen to my occupational calling. In my sophomore year I took a job at a dairy. I enjoyed the work immensely and decided I was going to become a dairyman. I pondered the thought for only a very short time, however, because once again, using earthly means, the Holy Spirit worked outside my closed-off heart to lead me.

Throughout the summer of 1976 various people said to me that I should become a minister or that I would make a good minister. People would make these comments out of the blue, and some of those who made such comments were virtual strangers. A cousin whom I saw an average of once a year, for example, said that I would make a good minister.

The Holy Spirit was guiding these people to make these comments to me, and these episodes weighed heavily on my mind. Finally I had to talk with someone about it. I took aside my best friend and told him all that had been going on, and I asked him whether he thought this could be God's calling me to the ministry. He advised me to have an open and receptive mind about the situation. That is not what I wanted to hear. I wanted to be told that I was an eccentric, weak-minded, off-the-wall fanatic. I tried to forget his advice, too, but soon after our talk I had my "Damascus Road" experience.

My friend was in the habit of coming over almost every night of the week, but he seldom came over during the afternoon, let alone a Sunday afternoon. To my surprise he dropped in on the Sunday afternoon following our talk. For the past week my mother had been trying to get me to listen to a tape she had bought from the Mount Hermon Christian Conference Center. As my friend and I were lazing about outside, doing nothing in particular, my mother approached us and asked us if we would listen to the tape since we had nothing better to do. I started a hesitant reply when my friend blurted out, "Why not? We're not doing anything."

On the tape the speaker told how he discovered God's will as to the college he should attend. He mentioned to several people, including some he did not know very well, that he was trying to choose a college. Every one of them unknowingly suggested the same college. The speaker said that he thought to himself at the time that there must have been a conspiracy, but people continued to suggest that particular college. Finally he concluded that if this was not the Holy Spirit's leading, then the Holy Spirit does not lead.

Through this tape the Holy Spirit gave me an example of how he showed someone else his will in the same way he was showing me his will for my life's work. After listening to the tape and discussing it, my friend and I entered the house, walked into the living room, and sat down where my parents and some relatives were visiting. We were talking about college when my uncle asked, "What are you going to learn for in college, to be a *Dominie?*" My friend and I looked at each other and laughed aloud. Farewell, Damascus!

A Slap in the Face

Just as I had to learn that I was not breaking ground for God when I began ministry in Uptown, so too I had to learn that I was not doing what God could not do or was not already doing there. God does not present himself to and exist only among Christians. Neither does God work only among Christians. Just as God prods my heart and leads me according to his will through physical and circumstantial means, so too he was prodding and leading the people of Uptown before I arrived on the scene. Just as we cannot possibly go where God has not been, when we arrive in a new place, we cannot do any work that God has not already been doing.

It must be extremely irritating to God when evangelists think that he has had to wait exclusively on them to deliver his Good News. This attitude and belief were exemplified to me by an evangelist who recently peeved me no end.

"How are you today, Brother?" he began the plastic conversation that I assumed was intended to convince me that he cares about me as a person.

"Well, as a matter of fact, I've got to qualify as one of the happiest people alive on the face of this earth today."

"Really?" he asked in astonishment. "Why's that?"

Did he ever set himself up!

"Because I am not my own, but belong—body and soul, in life and in death—to my faithful Savior Jesus Christ. He has fully paid for all my sins with his precious blood, and has set me free from the tyranny of the devil. He also watches over me in such a way that not a hair can fall from my head without the will of my God in heaven;

in fact, all things must work together for my salvation. Because I belong to him, Christ, by his Holy Spirit, assures me of eternal life and makes me wholeheartedly willing and ready from now on to live for him." (This was from the Heidelberg Catechism, Question and Answer 1.)

I had sensed from the outset of our dialogue that this fellow was fond of the "Kennedy approach" and was looking for an opening through which he could discharge his "Kennedy questions," positioned and ready for launch like spiritual warheads. I was certain that my heartfelt testimony, although memorized, would lead to a truce complete with disarmament and a joyful celebration between two children of God discovering that they shared the same chief.

No such providence.

"You know all the right answers, don't you," he stated indignantly while throwing me his calling card. "When you're ready for a *real* relationship with Jesus Christ, give me a call."

Like the apostle Paul, many of us are on the road to Damascus. We need a slap in the face to realize what is of God; a kick in the pants to recognize the activity of God prior to our arrival and during our tenure. In the same way that the evangelist was blind to God's presence in me, so I was blind to God's presence and activity in Uptown. God was in Uptown, as he was in all the rest of his world, busily working to transform and redeem all of culture.

Transforming Uptown

God's transforming work involves reconciling his image bearers to himself, but it also includes the redeeming of the relationships that his image bearers have with each other and with the world. God's redemptive work embraces our physical, political, economic, and social lives as well as our spiritual lives. Nowhere have I seen God manifest himself so clearly in this regard than in Uptown.

In this depressed and desperate neighborhood, the people refuse to do to one another what this country's rich, strong, talented, male-dominated aristocracy has done to them. Uptown is probably the single most racially and ethnically mixed neighborhood in the world. With few exceptions, this neighborhood exhibits unparalleled fellowship in suffering. The people of Uptown have gone a long way toward modifying the social and political structures of their community. They have not done so by envying a higher social class, nor by exaggerated esteem of the wealthy and their possessions of power, but by a new interpretation of life. By redefining success and including effort and selflessness in its criteria, they have become the envy of many who are materially better off. Such a miracle could only have come from a present and active God.

The strength of the bond of fellowship in suffering in Uptown never ceases to amaze me. On numerous occasions I have witnessed people giving away their last bite to eat because, although they have not eaten for a day, the person to whom they gave the food (often a person who is no more than a casual acquaintance) has not eaten for a longer time. Even the homeless youth of Uptown exhibit this social phenomenon. They provide each other with the hugs their parents never gave to them. The homeless youth protect, entertain, and provide for each other. Collectively they have become the family that eluded them in preadolescence. Such miracles could only have come from a present and active God.

It was an experience I had with one of these homeless youth in particular that led me to see that the community's fellowship in suffering even extends to such nontangible qualities as dignity, esteem, and respect. One night as I turned left onto Leland from Racine Street in my nightly walk among my parishioners, I encountered a group of nine young people who were hanging out on their usual porch. It had been just over two years since I first met these youth. Most of them are into drug dealing. They know that I know, but they refuse to deal directly in front of me. They will deal as close as ten yards away from me, but keep the goods hidden from my view. That's respect.

What Wayne did this particular night shows the extent of that respect. He was off to the side of this crowd of nine when I approached the group. Had I known what he was doing, I would have delayed my approach and greeting. He was off to the side because he didn't want me to see him smoking marijuana.

But I did not know this and went over to say hello and to shake his hand. Seeing me approaching, he immediately put the lit butt under his underarm to extinguish it. Not only did he not want to smoke it in front of me, but he also wanted to keep me from knowing that he was engaging in this bad and illegal habit. He knows I care about him, and he did not want to hurt me. And as he himself said when I told him that he did not have to burn his underarm on my account: "I don't care. I want to show you respect."

Additional evidence of God's transforming work in Uptown is a growing spirit of selflessness. This, too, I could demonstrate from the lives of many people. Even more remarkable, however, is finding selflessness within the local political and economic institutions. The community's alderman, for instance, despite the selfishness of most of Uptown's voters, is fighting to secure affordable housing for the community. And behind her are leaders in economic institutions who are willing to underwrite the housing when the alderman wins her battle.

Toward a Holistic Evangelism

The implications of this transformation for evangelism are monumental. Our brick-and-mortar churches are not bad places. In fact, they are good and necessary places if we can experience there the communion of the saints, benefit from mutual pastoral care and discipline, and be edified and equipped by the proclamation of the Word and participation in the sacraments. They are bad places, however, if they shut out those who are "outside" the church, labeling them "profane." If we consider certain people beneath us because of their morals or lifestyle, we are falsely supposing that a person must become religious before he or she can hear the gospel. If that had been the case, Christ would have passed by Zacchaeus, the Samaritan woman, and many others.

In evangelism we need to affirm the place of people in the

world. After all, although we are not to be *of* the world, God did command us to be *in* the world. It is in the world where people are most easily pointed to God, because it is in the world where people are, like God, concerned with thinking instead of thought, acting justly rather than with justice. People care more about *action* than about static *being*.

When asked about truth, the Old Testament Israelites would not begin a discussion on the ontology of God; rather, they would talk about Jehovah doing what he says he will do. It is outside the temple that evangelists can point out the faithfulness of an active God who keeps his word. As evangelists we are called to profaneness. Only outside the temple can we work actively with God to exhibit and exercise this truth.

To transform culture, God actively creates and reestablishes humanity—self-worth, respect, dignity, agapic love, and community—among his people. It makes sense, then, that effective ministry and evangelistic efforts will most often take place in a setting filled with a genuine sense of family and perhaps even some sense of covenant. In regard to established ministry, I suspect that this is not such an earthshakingly novel idea. With regard to evangelism, however, I suspect that if Uptown proves the validity of my hypothesis, we will have learned something significant and new. We will have learned that rather than working for conversions to create a new church, we need first to create a church out of which conversions might occur.

Those who understand the value of this approach are those who see God actively at work in all areas of life and in all parts of the world. Such an approach to evangelism is holistic and thus one most easily appreciated by those who see Christ as Transformer of Culture and not just as Redeemer of souls. In other words, I do not believe in a "souls-only" approach to evangelism. God is interested in the redemption, not only of souls, but of nature, bodies, minds, relationships, families, and communities. Salvation preached on street corners and through screen doors is often lopsided and, in some contexts, a misrepresentation of the Good News, for it covers only the spiritual aspect of our multifaceted lives.

A recent episode with the homeless youth of Uptown encouraged me in my efforts to establish a sense of trust, community, family, and even covenant with these young people. Because I reached out to these youth as whole persons, not just as souls, some very young kids turned to me as *their* pastor. Trixie (age eleven) told Valerie (twelve) about her friend Lei (fourteen), who had run away from home because of an abusive stepfather and now had nowhere to live. Valerie, who is a ward of the state and who also lives on the streets, told Trixie that she was sure "Father Mark" could be trusted to help. "Of course," Trixie exclaimed, " 'Father Mark' helped me after I ran away from home and lived on the streets, and he helped me to go back home to Mom."

Trixie and Valerie called the Night Ministry at 1:10 A.M., and since I was carrying a beeper, I was over and speaking with them and Lei in six minutes. I prefaced my questions to Lei by assuring her that she could trust me and that anything she said "can and will be held in confidence by me, as a minister, except information regarding intentions to harm yourself or another." These comments were interrupted by exclamations of reassurance from both Trixie and Valerie such as, "I told you so . . . Yes, he can be trusted . . . What did I tell you about *our* minister!"

These children have not yet come to a saving knowledge and faith in the Lord Jesus Christ. I agree that people can only be saved through the gospel; I am not a religious pluralist. It is my position, however, that for evangelistic efforts to be successful, in most cases the gospel not only *can* but *must* be communicated nonverbally as well as verbally. I have yet to see a person understand and exhibit forgiveness who has not first been shown and experienced forgiveness. I have yet to see a person understand and exhibit agapic love who has not first been *shown*—rather than *told about*—the love of Christ.

Profane evangelism takes the gospel to "unholy places." It embodies the gospel message in places and to people *outside* the church while recognizing that God is already active in those places. Furthermore, profane evangelism actually refuses to distinguish between "holy" and "unholy" places. Profane evangelism dares to make a sweeping claim: that God is the Master and Savior of all existence. Profane evangelism says that God cares as much about "a cup of cold water" being given to children like Trixie, Valerie, and Lei as about the Word being preached to them. And when a person is thirsty or homeless or sick or in prison, caring for his or her physical needs may take precedence over caring for their spiritual needs.

Evangelicals were a large part of the early ecumenical movement. After a time they concluded that the ecumenical movement's evangelistic mandate was being undermined and replaced by the so-called social gospel. Evangelicals became disillusioned with the ecumenical movement when it moved, as the evangelicals themselves concluded, toward a Christlike world rather than toward the evangelism of the world.

If my theology of evangelism is biblical and therefore tenable, then clearly, evangelicals have created a false dichotomy. Movement toward a Christlike world *is* the evangelism of the world. The holistic approach in evangelistic outreach and in the Christian's everyday living is a *sine qua non*, first of all, for the well-founded, born-again Christian. The Christian's faith, although itself freely given, requires responsible stewardship by the recipient. Faith and works are like two sides of one coin. Christian action is the necessary counterpart to faith, and faith-works must be the formula for our salvation. As James wrote, "You see that a person is justified by what he does and not by faith alone" (2:24). Faith perfected by Christian action is also the point of Jesus' parable about the foolish and wise builders (Luke 6:46–49).

The holistic approach to evangelism and to everyday Christian living is essential to effective outreach. A solely verbal evangelistic approach fails to reveal God as he has revealed himself; namely, as sovereign in all areas of life. Paul recognized the pervasiveness of the effects of sin and the need for an all-encompassing salvation when he wrote:

> We know that the whole creation has been groaning as in the pains of childbirth right up to the present time. Not only so, but we ourselves,

who have the firstfruits of the Spirit, groan inwardly as we wait eagerly for our adoption as sons, the redemption of our bodies" (Rom. 8:22–23).

A solely verbal evangelistic approach is usually a "souls-only" approach and is therefore in most contexts, not only ineffective, but also inherently heretical. A "souls-only" approach denies God's ubiquity and sovereign activity in his world and is thus unchristian, unbiblical, ungodly—and unconscionable.

I believe this false dichotomy of the one *Logos* is Satan's No. 1 ploy for sabotaging the church in North America today. Both leading someone to Christ and discipling Christians by means of the verbal *half* of the *Logos* alone is analogous to selling a car without a motor. One's ability to sell is greatly diminished, and for those who do buy, that which was meant to fill a void in their lives is less than enough. The ministry of the Word, including discipling people in Christian living, must be the crowning work of holistic outreach in ministry. By mentioning both the "Word" *and* "discipling people in Christian living" we avoid falling into the trap of making a false dichotomy between Word and deed, both of which are essential to the *Logos*.

If God wanted us to know more about his essence he would have told us more. Our quests for an ontological Jesus are counterproductive. Throughout the history of redemption God has revealed himself to us almost exclusively in terms of what he does. Could it be that God revealed so little of his essence in order to avoid the human quest for an individualistic, personal, confined, and limited "I-Thou" relationship? Could it be that God revealed so much of his activity in order to encourage the human quest for a communal and action-oriented "I-You" relationship in which we work alongside each other and with other human beings?

The point of departure in our evangelistic efforts has to be affirming where God already is and what he is already doing well in society *before* we get there. Then we must show God to the world, not as a historic and static entity, but as a God who is present and actively working right now.

Maybe in order to keep us off the road to Damascus we should give God a new name. "God" raises concerns of ontology, of God's essence, instead of giving us a picture of his activity. Perhaps we should call God "Precipitator" or "Conductor" or "Dispatcher" instead. At any rate, it is my hope and prayer that God will use this book to open the eyes of those who are unable to see his presence and activity in his world and so avert those who have been traveling the road to Damascus.

Chapter 3

On the Road to Nineveh

"So, you're a minister, huh?" asked the lanky, long-faced, Lincoln look-alike.

"Yes, I am," I answered in an exaggerated, monotone voice. My intuition told me that if a Fahrenheit could be correlated with this man's anger, mercury would soon shoot out his ears. My intentionally monotonous voice was a futile attempt to portray myself as a coward and give him the illusion that the power of his covert threat far exceeded his wildest calculation, and so give him pause.

Maybe next time.

More red in the face than before, he roared, "So what the hell is a minister doing in this type of neighborhood at two in the morning?"

Now *my* anger was beginning to surface. "In the first place, whether I am a gigolo or a mechanic or a minister, I am entitled to walk any streets of any neighborhood at any time. As for your question, I am working."

"You're a real *smart*-mouth minister too, aren't you? I ought to wring your little semi-divine neck!"

This guy was beginning to worry me. He was starting to demonstrate that he had at least a modicum of intelligence to go with his wrath. I also could have kicked myself for hopelessly confusing the issue. Did "Abe" want to wring my neck because I was a smart-mouth or because he found something inherently distasteful about ministers? He had forced my hand, so I tried the direct approach.

"Is there something about my being a minister that makes you angry?

"No. Well yes, that is, if you *are* a minister. I have my doubts. But if you are a minister, you're not supposed to be in a neighborhood like this. Especially at this hour."

I played dumb. "What's wrong with this neighborhood?"

Abe's mercury started to rise again. "Look over there, man!" he commanded. "Don't you see those whores? Look over there! Don't you see those drunks? Look over there! Don't you see those 'druggies'? Take a whiff. Can't you smell the booze and the bo [marijuana] in the air?"

Carrying out a ritual I had picked up from my good friend, Father Depaul Genske, I tensed the fingers of my right hand and thrice pounded them into my forehead while thrice scolding myself: "Thick . . . thick . . . thick!"

To clarify myself, I then said, "So what concerns you about my presence in this neighborhood, and at this hour, is not what the neighborhood might do to me or the church, but what I or the church might do to the neighborhood."

At least I thought I was clearing the air. He first denied and then repeated what I had said in a different and—I must admit—more understandable way. "No, man! What I am saying is that you church people have no right to tell us how to live. If I want religion or feel the need to make a confession, I'll let you know. Know what I mean?"

I was 99 percent sure that I knew what he meant. But once again taking my Bible too literally, I left the ninety-nine to secure the one. "Let me see. You are uncomfortable with my presence because you might wish to behave in certain ways and engage in certain behaviors of which the church does not approve."

I am not certain, but this time I thought for sure that I saw mercury spouting from Abe's ears. "No shit! Get the hell out of here! If you're concerned about me, go to your church and pray for me!"

Body and Soul

This episode is typical of conversation and encounters I have had with scores of my parishioners in Uptown. These encounters hold the primary key to the question of why the church in North America seems largely irrelevant. The key is our lack of profaneness. That is, the church has become irrelevant insofar as it portrays, by both word and action—or inaction—that God neither exists outside nor is interested in what goes on outside our temples.

If I had allowed the church to mislead me into believing that God is only interested in prayer and praise and worship and inspirational things, then I too would be upset with him and any of his followers who impinged on my turf. I do not particularly care to have the plumber hanging around my apartment when I neither called nor have need of one. Non-Christians view God as an intrusive nuisance because the church has given them the impression that God is not interested in their personal thoughts, feelings, interests, hobbies, or relationships—let alone in their struggle for survival. God, they think, is interested only in their souls, not their bodies.

The false dichotomy between body and soul that church people have created by evangelizing souls alone has become a grave stumbling-block to many would-be Christians. Consider another conversation typical of many between my parishioners and me.

"Hi, Father. 'S up?" Jorge greeted me on the street one night.

"Oh, nothin' to it really. See you're still totin' bo [smoking marijuana]."

"Yeah. Well, you know. I don't smoke that much but, well

(sigh), you know, life can be a bitch and then a fella has to loos'n up some. You know!

"Yes, life can be real difficult at times, can't it?"

Jorge stared contemplatively at the ground for a while. After relighting his marijuana butt he said, "At least I know that everything is going to be all right in the end."

"Really?" I asked, trying desperately not to sound too surprised.

"Oh yeah!" Jorge declared. "When I die I'm making a beeline for heaven." Pointing straight up, Jorge grinned confidently.

I could not help but probe. "Your assurance is inspiring. I would hate to do anything to ruin that, but do you mind if I ask you a few questions about it?"

"No. Go 'head."

"Smoking bo is illegal, right?"

"Right."

"Don't you think God is displeased when we break the law?"

"When we break *his* laws," Jorge said with a wave of his hand.

"Well, then, what about the damage to the body that marijuana is reputed to do. Don't you think harming our bodies displeases God?"

"What's the big deal?" Jorge shrugged his shoulders. "When I'm done with my body, God can have my soul."

Purchasing God's "Goodies"

A shockingly large number of people in Uptown have the same beliefs as Jorge. Yet, given the church's message that God is interested in salvaging only a part of his creation, Jorge's beliefs, although sad, are sensible. Again, our false dichotomy in evangelistic work sorely needs rethinking. Until our evangelism makes it clear that God is ubiquitous, until it illustrates that God is concerned with more than people's souls, God will continue to lose those whom the church has led to believe that there is a certain time and place for everything, including God.

Surely God calls us to his temple. But he set aside only one day for it. Six days we are called to be outside the temple. Yet most of us act on Monday as though we are still in the temple and that it is the only place where we can come to God. The same dichotomy that so badly confuses and hinders would-be Christians has the same negative ramifications for church people. Because we think that God is confined to our temples and limits his transforming work of redemption to the souls who enter into them, we fall into the trap of believing that salvation can be purchased.

It happens all the time. Despite Martin Luther and the Reformation, many Protestants are busy going about trying to purchase salvation. Our modern-day attempts are just better hidden than in the past—couched in all the right ecclesiastical jargon, framed by all the right theological idioms, and reinforced by all the right weekly rituals. Many of us have fallen into the trap of believing that salvation is the reward of those with the *most correct* understanding of the Scriptures.

This is why I did not find it incredible to hear a man in Uptown ask me, literally, how many dollars it would take to get salvation for his two-year-old daughter. To him, many church people appeared to be purchasing their salvation. "I don't care whether I am saved or not," this father said. "It's probably too late for me. The cost would be too great. I just want my daughter saved. She is all I live for anymore." (The less the sin, the less the cost? Where did he get that idea?)

Holistic evangelism is more important than ever before. The behavior of many institutionalized churches has led an appalling number of people to believe that—like their having to jump all the hoops of the social worker in order to gain access to government goods—they must jump all the hoops of the church to gain access to the "goodies" of God.

Even worse than feeling they must jump the hoops is the feeling of these parishioners that they cannot even approach God. To them he seems so terribly far removed. Here, too, I ask: Has the church acted in such a way as to lead others to believe that they must go to a special place and that God must be properly charmed to be approached?

By our taking the church to the people rather than getting people into a church, many in Uptown are discovering that God is at-large and only a prayer-length away.

"Let me ask you something, Mark," requested Arrow, a seventeen-year-old American Indian, "I've known you for quite a while, but we never had a really serious conversation together yet."

"You've earned that right," I quipped encouragingly.

"All right . . . Okay . . . All right. I'm not that bad of a person, I guess. Well, look, I ain't gonna lie to you. I drink and pop [pills]; and, okay, I do sell some bo. Does that mean I'll go to hell?"

"Probably not."

"Those are sins, aren't they?" Arrow asked incredulously.

"Yes, those are sins, Arrow; but there is no person who has ever lived who is without sin—except, of course, Jesus Christ."

"Then I guess we're all going to hell, right?" concluded Arrow with a wave of his hand, as though all hope were gone.

"Wrong! Because Jesus never sinned, he is the only one who never had to die. He chose to be tortured and die anyway, though, and in that way he paid for the sins of all the rest of us."

In a rare expression of emotion and with deep compassion, Arrow blurted out, "That's not fair!"

"That brings up a good point, Arrow. When you ask Jesus to make his death count for your sins, you might also thank him that life's not fair."

"I'll do that," Arrow promised, his eyes bright with new understanding and new hope.

A Dichotomous View of Evangelism

God is calling us to Nineveh. On the road to Nineveh, the prophet Jonah tried to sidestep his calling many times and in various ways. He could not figure out why God wanted him to go to Nineveh. Couldn't the Ninevites see that if they wanted Jehovah and his gift of salvation, the land of Israel was the place to be?

Jonah had a very basic attitude problem. He did not think that anyone outside the nation of Israel deserved *his* Lord's grace. Jonah held a dichotomous view of evangelism that is analogous to the dichotomous evangelistic perspective of many church people today. Jonah fell into the trap of thinking that Jehovah existed for Israel rather than Israel for Jehovah.

Jonah had to learn that salvation is in Jehovah's hands. He had to learn that God's plan of salvation was not confined to Israel. Jonah had to learn that God's plan for salvation was designed for a whole lot more than Israel. Jonah had to learn that Jehovah did not treasure Israel for itself, as a nation, but for what Israel was—an instrument for redemption of all the earth. When God explained to Jonah his interest in Nineveh, he did not just mention his concern for souls. In Jonah 4:11 God mentions people *and cattle and the city itself.*

God's call to Jonah extends to us. We have learned that our dichotomous view of evangelism, our belief that God is interested in salvaging only a part of what he so creatively brought into existence and so carefully sustains, has been a stumbling-block to both ourselves and would-be Christians. Like Jonah, we are called to bring together again in fruitful tension the two parts of our fabricated dichotomy, both of which are within the transformation design God has for the redemption of all his creation.

Jonah, the Suburban Pastor

As I was making my rounds on Magnolia Street between Wilson and Leland avenues, eight youths on the steps of an abandoned building called to me. They wanted to figure out more about who I was and what I was up to. The discussion soon moved to their showing me how much they knew about the Bible and religion. One youth began telling me about Jonah and the whale, and less than midway he realized he had forgotten most of it. He asked me to recount the story for him. I gladly obliged.

"Jonah," I began, "was a minister in the suburb of Wheaton. He had a delightful job. The contributions of his parishioners exceeded three times the called-for budget every year. He had assistant pastors to teach the young peoples' classes and to make most of the hospital visits and take care of the marriages and funerals and other such things. Jonah was especially glad that he didn't have to deal with the young people of the church. In his opinion, the young people were just a bunch of rebellious brats who couldn't care less whether or not there is a God, because all they cared about was what they can get out of life. Jonah was only expected to provide top-notch sermons on Sundays. And he was the best. People came from miles around to hear his sermons. 'Life couldn't be better,' Jonah thought to himself. 'I think I will stay at this church until I retire.'

"But one day God spoke to Jonah in his dreams. God said: 'I want you to go and call a faithful people for me out of the city of Chicago. I want you to focus especially on reaching out to and helping the young people of that city. Pay special attention to my homeless children. Do not hinder them, for to such belongs the kingdom of heaven.' To Jonah this dream was a nightmare. He went to Chicago all right. But he went to Chicago to board 'Old Silversides,' the historic submarine that was on its way to Muske-gon, Michigan, for display.

"It really wasn't that Jonah was afraid to try something else or to work hard in the ministry. He was willing to make those kinds of sacrifices. But where God had gone too far, according to Jonah, was when he asked him to go and minister in Chicago. In Jonah's opinion, the people of Chicago did not deserve to share the same God that he had. 'Why should the people of Chicago share the joys, the privileges, and the blessings that my own people have?' Jonah asked himself. 'The blacks are too lazy to work for a better life and move to the suburbs.' (Jonah denied that the suburban whites would refuse to accept blacks on their turf.) 'The Indians and Spanish peoples like the way they live,' he concluded to himself, 'because compared to where they came from, they already live in luxury.' (He didn't realize that the Indians and Spanish peoples had never been given the educational and occupational opportunities that would enable them to enjoy a few more of God's good gifts.) Jonah also concluded that Orientals kept to themselves and didn't want any help. (It never occurred to him that the Oriental people were never asked if they needed or desired help with anything.)

"The bottom line in all this, however, is that Jonah felt that God had given him the exclusive rights to the key that unlocks the door to a fulfilling life that lasts forever. You will notice that never once did it cross Jonah's mind that blacks, Hispanics, Indians, and Orientals had something to offer him. Jonah felt that the people of Chicago had no right to share the goodies that God had given him and his people. Jonah concluded that the people of Chicago were an unworthy people and that sharing with them was out of the question.

"So Jonah hopped on 'Old Silversides' and headed for Muskegon, Michigan, to run away from the task God had called him to do. Actually, Jonah had Norton Shores in mind, a suburb of Muskegon that reminded him of Wheaton.

"Now, the part of the story I'm sure you kids are dying to hear. Cutting its way across Lake Michigan, 'Old Silversides' got caught up in a nasty storm that threatened the old submarine. God had caused this storm specifically to teach Jonah a lesson. One of the sailors decided that if God can make a storm to teach someone on the ship a lesson, then he could also use the game of spin-the-bottle to help them know who the culprit was.

"The men (there were no women aboard the ship) all sat around in a circle on the deck of the ship. One of the sailors spun the bottle as hard as he could, and sure enough, when the bottle came to a standstill, its wide mouth stood pointing accusingly in the direction of Jonah. So, as you know, Jonah was thrown overboard. As he sank to the bottom of the lake, his life flashed before his eyes. He thought for sure he was dead meat. When he hit bottom, he said what he thought would be his last words: 'At least I didn't have to go to Chicago.'

"Just then a very large fish swallowed Jonah. Now a lot of people say it was a whale, but I've looked at this story in the Hebrew language in which it was originally written and, I assure you, it was not a whale. It was just a really big fish. That makes more sense anyway, since you and I both know that whales don't live in Lake Michigan. Inside the large fish Jonah knew that it was God who brought the fish along to save him. Now that fish ate a lot of garbage, and it really stunk inside. God uses a lot of different ways to get us to ask for forgiveness, and this time he used a smelly fish. Jonah couldn't stand the smell anymore and cried out, 'All right, all right, all right! I'm sorry, I'm sorry, I'm sorry! I'll do anything you say, Lord!"

"Jonah asked for it; he got it. God made Jonah wait for three days to give him a taste of his own medicine. Jonah began vomiting because of the smell inside that fish. This made the fish throw up too. God caused the fish to spit up Jonah near Gary, Indiana, where rumor has it that, because of the waste of the steel mills, Jonah was actually the first person in history to have walked on water.

"Anyway, Jonah grudgingly made his way back to Chicago and began the ministry God had called him to. What made him even more mad, though, is that he was successful. But to make a long story not quite so long, Jonah learned that when God first made people, he took the first batch out of the oven too soon and they were too raw. Those are us white people. The second batch of people God kept in too long, and they got burnt. Those are the black people like you, Shenina, Kareem, and Roshana. But most of the people God did just right. Those are the people like you, Chai, Ling, Maria, Tito, and Horse.

"All kidding aside, God taught Jonah that everlasting life and happiness is not just the privilege of one select group of people. God offers his gifts to everyone. And God has been good enough to teach me this too. That is why I am happy to be here in Chicago and working with homeless kids—because homeless kids especially deserve help to get the loving parents and nice homes that God wishes for everyone to have."

The Sound of One Hand Clapping

If God is concerned about the transformation and redemption of cattle, then he is concerned in the same way for all his creation. If God is concerned about the transformation and redemption of

cities, then he is concerned in the same way for his image bearers—
no matter who they are. God has privileged us with the opportunity
to be his hands and feet here on earth and to be co-workers with
him and with each other in his great plan for the transformation and
redemption of the world. If we refuse to leave our temples and
exercise our privilege to work alongside God in his world, he will
work his way and realize his will without us.

It is my passion and prayer that Word and deed can once again
be reunited into the one *Logos* from which they originated. To me
this equals a biblical faithfulness and a twentieth- and twenty-first-
century relevancy that will take the fear out of evangelism for the
layperson and provide us with a solid principle, complete with
guidelines, for being what we are called to be: profane evangelists
on the road to Nineveh. We need both hands—both Word and
deed—to clap. If we refuse to heed our calling, then no matter how
much noise we make in church, we will be to God's ears like the
sound of one hand clapping.

Part Two

EXHIBITING PROFANE EVANGELISM: Passing God's Bar Exam

"My prayer is not that you take them out of the world but that you protect them from the evil one."

—John 17:15

Chapter 4

Flying Nun of the Eighties

To show that God exists and acts outside the temple, to show that God cares about every facet of life, Christians—who are in but not of the world—must be careful how they live among those who are in but not of the kingdom.

How, for an example, can we expect people to believe that God is a patient, long-suffering, and persevering God when we are often fervently, and sometimes violently, pushing God upon them? If a conversion is not imminently forthcoming, many take it personally, write the person off as hopeless, and rush on to the next potential convert. Under those circumstances, what in our behavior reveals God as patient, long-suffering, and persevering?

A Year and Seven Months

No sooner had I stepped out of my car for another evening among my parishioners than I heard a small voice calling my name.

I was not immediately able to identify where on the crowded sidewalk the voice came from. Several more calls were necessary before I was able to identify the voice as that of "Madam Hook," queen of the Gaylords, also known as "MaH." I had been seeing MaH around for a year and seven months, and for a year and seven months it was the same old story: MaH pretended all was well.

This time, while leaving her room for denial, I also gave her the opportunity to covertly admit to the areas in her life where she needed help. I showed her some condoms and invited her to take them if they would be helpful in reducing the risk of contracting AIDS. MaH accepted them, thereby all but admitting to activity in prostitution. I showed her some little bottles of bleach and invited her to take them if they would be helpful for cleansing any needle works she might share and so reduce the risk of catching AIDS. MaH accepted them also, thereby all but admitting to still being hooked on cocaine. Yet, verbally I received the same old message.

"I'm really doing quite well now, though, Father. I'm doing better than I have for a long, long time."

"Okay," I replied in a yielding tone of voice, "but if you ever want to hear about some good programs to help you kick that drug habit . . ."

"No, really! Everything is fine." MaH forced her lips to smile, but her eyes betrayed feelings of guilt.

"I'm glad to hear that, MaH. I just want you to know that I care about you and that you can come to me for anything. . . . Oh, that reminds me, I've been intending to tell you about a marvelous group of women who have been extremely successful in helping women get out of prostitution and into safer types of occupations."

"Okay," MaH responded with a hint of impatience.

"Some other time, huh?" I took my cue and began to walk away. Over my shoulder, as I continued to walk, I yelled as earnestly as possible, "It's really good to see you again, MaH, and to see you doing so well! Take care."

Within minutes I heard footsteps scurrying to catch up to me. "Mark, Mark, slow up a minute, would you!" Breathlessly MaH continued, "I'm tired of lying to you, Mark. I didn't mean to lie to you. It was just that I didn't want you to worry or feel bad about me. But you're the only one out here who has really loved me and cared about me, and if I'm going to change, you are the only one I trust to help me. I'm not doing so well. I have no place to call home. I exchange sex for a place to stay at night. And just look at my hand! It's all swelled up because I couldn't find the vein with the needle right away. I am into cocaine as 'tall' as ever. Who are these women who help us prostitutes?"

A year and seven months! That's how long it took to establish trust, rapport, and belief in the purity of my motives; in short, it took a year and seven months before MaH was able to believe the message that Christ was delivering through me. It may take even longer before MaH understands and accepts Jesus' complete message to her, but she is on the way. Nearly every time we get together now, she requests, "Tell me more about Jesus' walk among the women in prostitution while he was here on earth." More often than not, I tell MaH about Jesus' contemporary walks with them.

Slowly, But Surely

Closely associated with our need to walk patiently among those we wish to evangelize is our need to walk slowly.

Betty had been living with the father of her child ever since the last weeks of her pregnancy. The two never got along. Betty has a drinking problem and struggles between the urge to party and the urge to be a responsible mother. She defends both equally. Her live-in, John, is very insecure, and he mentally and physically abuses both Betty and their infant son. John does not want Betty to work or to get on the welfare roll because he is afraid of Betty's becoming independent. He feels a need to keep her totally dependent on him, and he does not stop short of threatening the life of ten-month-old John Junior, should Betty ever desert him. John is also on cocaine. Both of them avidly defend and protect their vices, and both justify their vices by discounting the other's parental fitness: "Sure I party from time to time, but at least I see to it that John Junior is changed, fed, and in good hands."

On one of my nocturnal swings through Uptown's most notorious bars, I spied Betty in the Paper Nickel, in tears and with a black eye. Several times previously, she had opened up to me, but she never trusted me enough to open up sufficiently for me to help her. On this particular night she "bottomed out," and I was able to be of some initial help to her. Since Betty lent herself in prostitution periodically, I felt it was legitimate to take her to a hospitality house for women in prostitution. There she could get the additional support of a female counselor with a lot more experience than me in regard to women who trap themselves in an abusive lifestyle. I figured that, if nothing else, Betty would at least learn that there are other people who understand and care and are very willing to help.

Betty agreed to go. At the hospitality house a woman named Maggie counseled Betty with me. During the course of the succeeding three hours, Betty learned and clearly understood that she was following a pattern of self-abuse taught by her mother. Betty's mother socialized her into the belief that, without any regard to herself, a woman's worth in life revolves around taking care of her husband first and then her children. Betty's mother catered to an abusive husband and demanded that her children cater to an abusive father. Betty was taught that children are to be neglected so long as the demands of an abusive father remain unmet.

During the counseling session, whenever she was asked what positive steps she might take to begin caring for herself, Betty always talked of caring for her son first. After affirming her love and concern for her son, I asked, "Are you not yourself worth these positive steps?" I asked her this question several times, and Betty consistently responded, "No, I'm not, only my son."

The counseling also helped Betty to see that, because she was taught this pattern of self-abuse, she continued to go to men who needed her. In other words, she went to men who were dependent on her because she had never learned that her own life and being were worth more than that. When asked whether she would ever go to a man who did not need her but who *wanted* her just because he liked her, she could not comprehend either the sense of being with such a man or what that relationship might look like or mean.

One additional thing we taught Betty on this night was, again, something we were able to help her comprehend, but unable to help her actually execute. We taught her about alternatives in conflict management, about how to respond to John without either feeding his anger or giving in to him. Maggie asked Betty to consider how she replies to John—yelling, ranting, losing control, screaming, raving, threatening, jumping up and down—and then to consider how her favorite actress or actor might respond to John's threats. After a moment of reflection, Betty smiled for the first time that night as she told us that Angie Dickinson would respond in a firm but composed voice, "Johnny, you're entitled to your opinion, but lay one hand on me and John Junior and I will be but a fond memory in the dark recesses of your mind." Maggie then asked Betty to envision herself replying to John in such a manner and asked her what would happen. Betty replied that John would be shocked and speechless—and then she smiled broadly for the second time that evening.

Naturally Betty was still concerned that John would beat her even if she spoke in such a manner. Since she insisted on going home at least one more time, we reassured her that John would see a Betty who was self-confident and taking steps to be self-reliant—and without him if need be. It would be John's last beating. Finally the ball would be in John's court.

At 2:00 A.M. I drove Betty home through the neon streets of Chicago's north side. For once the streets were as quiet as the woman sitting in the seat beside me.

"Penny for your thoughts?" I broke the silence.

Betty was all smiles now, excited at discovering for the first time that she had power and control over her own life.

"Why didn't you do this for me a long time ago, Mark?" she asked.

"Why didn't you allow me to help you to help yourself a long time ago, Betty?" I asked, rephrasing and returning the question.

"Oh," Betty exclaimed, "now I understand what you meant all those times when I asked you what you could do for me and you turned around and asked me, 'What will you allow me to help you do for yourself?'"

There were many times when I was tempted to push and preach at Betty. I am glad I didn't, for I'm convinced it would have been counterproductive. Betty had had enough pushed on her in her life. She had to first be shown God acting in her life before she would be receptive to the verbal half of the one *Logos*. We Christians do not do nearly enough preparation for evangelistic work. When guilt looms large and we finally get around to evangelism, then we are always in too big a hurry. Church people always believe in elaborate preparations . . . for everything else.

Why do we think we can evangelize without preparation? Don't we need to prepare not only ourselves, but also those to whom we witness? One might argue that time is short and so we need to pound the Word into people's heads. Is it not equally logical to contend that since Jesus is tarrying so that not one might be lost, we can afford to engage in longer-range evangelism efforts that reveal the Word in its fullness and therefore result in fewer phonies and more disciples? In 1 Peter 3, the apostle Peter does not suggest that people with unbelieving spouses nag them; he encourages those in such a predicament to set an example for their spouses in order to win them over. Slowly, but surely.

Treading Softly

We must wait patiently and walk slowly to show the presence of a long-suffering God to our parishioners. Besides being patient and slow, however, we must also be soft. We must present ourselves softly, or humbly, so that we may truly empathize with our parishioners.

Every person who opens up to us wants to know if we sincerely share in his or her joys or burdens. If we merely say so, the person remains unconvinced. We need to be so humble, especially in our conversations, that we allow our parishioners to take center stage, and ourselves work backstage to help them. As humble messengers we correctly deliver the message of a God who cares about his people. But if we choose to be haughty couriers of the Lord's will, we will deliver a false and harmful message of an arrogant God who makes demands irrespective of where one is or what one is doing. Whenever I take on the role of haughty courier, I find myself having to say something, rather than having something to say. That is the substance of my error in the following story.

Wilson Avenue between Broadway and Magnolia harbors one of the scores of mini-skid rows scattered around the city. Here live many of the stereotypical down-and-outers. And here, for a couple of hours each night, there moves graciously among the lost and dispossessed a remarkable fifty-one-year-old woman named Karen. Seemingly oblivious to the dirt and smells, she sits beside each person, talking for ten to fifteen minutes with each one. Karen's gift is a heavenly balm of respect and love. In addition to giving the dispossessed someone to talk to, Karen takes messages to and from their friends in jail.

When I first came to Uptown, before I had established myself and earned the right to be on their turf, I was anxious to have my parishioners own the ministry as much as possible. I wanted to establish elders and deacons, so to speak. I wished to build others up and bring them into the ministry. Karen seemed to be a prime candidate for this, for God's presence with her was obvious to me. I figured that all I would need to do was correlate her work with God's.

One night I talked to Karen at length after she had made the rounds with her skid row friends. I commended Karen for her work and generally sought to build her up. Unknown to me, on that particular night Karen had been salving her friends' emotional wounds, inflicted by another "evangelist" who had gone through the neighborhood before me, preaching the whereabouts and activities of God in some temple with a funny name and liberally applying salt to the people's wounds. I mention this only to accentuate my own unpreparedness and pride as I began this ministry.

"Yep, Karen, it's quite a ministry you got going here."

Her reply was immediate, harsh, and humbling. "I ain't no

damn minister! You don't hear me going around and preaching at people, do you?"

Blue Jeans and Clerical Collars

The Christian's appearance also has a lot to do with how a community perceives the presence of God. Once a homeless kid told me he might be more interested in God if he were "not such an old fogy who listens to outdated music and insists on ties and slacks." Then he noticed my old, faded blue jeans and said, "I guess he's lightening up some, huh?" I also choose to wear a clerical collar in the community that I have been called to evangelize. Complemented by blue jeans, it is usually helpful. In a few instances, however, it has led others to perceive God inaccurately. The following is a good example.

"Hello, Barbara."

No response.

"HELLO, Barbara!"

Still no response. Wait a minute . . . "Oh, hi, Mark!"

"You okay, Barbara?"

"Yeah . . . (long pause) . . . it's just that—"

"Yes?"

"It's just that . . . well, you make me nervous."

"Is there anything I can do to make you less nervous?" I asked, perplexed.

"I don't think so," Barbara responded, as distant as when our conversation began.

"But I really feel bad, Barbara. If you would just be so kind as to tell me what it is about me that makes you feel uncomfortable, then I would be a very happy man, because then I would know if it is something that makes other people uncomfortable too, and then I could change whatever it is. I would feel real bad if I made other people feel nervous around me too."

"I don't think it makes other people feel nervous."

"I still feel bad if it makes you nervous, Barbara."

"I'm sorry," Barbara said, finally expressing emotion. "I don't mean to make you feel bad or anything."

"Then you'll help me?" I asked, trying to capitalize on her opening.

"Yes . . . well . . . no . . . I mean, I don't think what makes me nervous makes other people nervous."

"I think it does," I stated, admittedly crossing the fine line between capitalizing on and manipulating the opportunity.

"How do you know?" Barbara asked in disbelief. "You don't even know what it is that makes me nervous."

"Sure I do," I declared with exaggerated confidence, "I remind you of your third-to-the-last boyfriend, whom you killed and threw in a dumpster in 'Death Alley' and thought no one knew about."

She laughed hysterically. "Don't be silly, it's your collar. Oops!"

"My collar?"

"I'm sorry, Mark, but yes. When you have your collar on around me, I'm very uneasy. I feel sorta, well, spooked. See, I have some pretty bad, I guess you would call them sinful, habits. When you're around I see how good you are, and then I start to thinkin' about how bad I am, and, well, I get scared, like, well, like . . . God's gonna get me."

In Barbara's case, until I counteracted with pastoral care, the collar gave a false impression of God. To her the collar represented a God who was present only when my collar was present, and it represented favoritism from God. My collar further symbolized to Barbara a God who, if ever active in his creation, was only supernaturally active. After a few months and several counseling sessions with Barbara, I took my "tongue depressor" out (as I had taken to calling the plastic tab in the neck of my shirt ever since that conversation with Barbara), gave it to her, and invited her to wear it. I had overestimated the efficacy of my counseling. Barbara screamed, leaped to her feet, and ran for the exit of the Paper Nickel Bar. Fortunately she continued to allow me some space. Eventually I was able to redeem myself and exorcise her fear, if the hug I recently received from her while I was wearing the collar indicates anything.

An Agapic Hug

Besides being careful about our appearance, treading softly, walking slowly and surely, and waiting patiently, we need to love agapically. We need to love our parishioners in a giving way, expecting nothing in return, not even a corresponding love or respect. Agapic love is love without demands. It is a love characterized by giving and esteeming.

Weeping Willow is a forty-one-year-old American Indian woman. She often asked me to pray for her. I always agreed, but did not ask her what exactly she wanted me to pray for. I wanted her to have to tell me. This way she would begin to own up to her problems and, I hoped, begin to take responsibility for them.

In The Sousery, a bar under the El (Chicago's elevated train tracks), I often sit alone at a booth big enough for four. This way, those who wish to talk to a minister-type can recognize a nonverbal invitation. This invitation also leaves room for those who need someone to talk with, but who do not care to talk about matters of faith. This approach, or nonapproach, moreover, weeds out the kinds of people who invent problems or who merely pretend that they are ready to deal with real problems.

It was to this booth that Weeping Willow came when she was ready to name her problem and take some responsibility for it. She told me about her three boys, whom she loved very much. She had given them all she could and had helped them in every way possible. Still, two of them were in jail—one of them unjustly, she maintained. The third son, White Wing, was about to go to court. Weeping Willow believed that he was falsely accused, too, but did admit he had been leading a less-than-wholesome lifestyle.

None of this is what was really bothering Weeping Willow, however. Like his two brothers before him, White Wing was asking his mother for financial help. His mother intuitively knew that it would not be good to give him any more money; yet she feared it meant she was an inadequate and unloving mother. She was homeless and broke because of her three boys, yet believed that she was the one who had failed them. She also *needed* to believe these things because she was a practicing alcoholic at the time, and alcoholics usually have a psychological need for some kind of self-flagellation.

I helped Weeping Willow do three things for herself as we sat and talked in The Sousery. First and most important, I listened. This was a brand-new experience for Weeping Willow. No one had ever listened to her before with other than enlightened self-interest, so I helped her to see that she was worthwhile in and of herself and therefore worthy of being heard. Several times Weeping Willow suggested that she was wasting my time and hinted that she should leave so I could do "something important." I begged her to stay.

"Why don't I just get going so you can talk to some of these other people?" she asked.

"Why don't you just stay? I enjoy talking to you," I responded.

"You make me feel so good!"

"I guess," I replied. "I believe this is the first time I've ever seen a smile on your face." Her smile broadened in response.

Weeping Willow showed embarrassment and shame at feeling so good. I told her frankly that she had nothing to be ashamed of, and I backed it up by telling her that she should feel free to call me at the office at any time and that I would meet her for coffee at any time and talk with her a whole lot more. This led to more smiles and even tears.

"You really care about me, don't you? You would really make a special trip just to go for coffee with me, wouldn't you? You make me feel so good!"

Second, I helped Weeping Willow to see that she judged her worth by her children—what they did, where they were at, and what they thought of her.

"But if I love them, I have to help them."

"You've done more than is required of any parent."

"But White Wing might have to go to jail. Shouldn't I help?"

"White Wing needs to learn to fly on his own now. (Happily

she didn't catch my ill-timed pun.) White Wing is a man now. He is responsible for his own actions. If he has to go to jail, there is nothing you can do to get him out of it. It is *his* fault, *not yours.*"

"But I love him."

"The most loving thing you can do for White Wing now is to let him accept the consequences and learn that he is responsible for his own actions. Now it is time for you to learn to love yourself."

We discussed this idea at length. It was a grueling task to get a second opinion admitted alongside the other that was tattooed into her mind. "Geronimo!" Weeping Willow exclaimed an hour and twenty minutes later. She boldly summarized what she thought I was driving toward. "You mean that my kids will learn to love and care for themselves when I learn to do the same for myself."

Third, perhaps for the same reason that Weeping Willow had never learned that her sons' mistakes were their responsibility, neither had she learned to accept responsibility for her own actions. During our conversation she had repeatedly asked for prayer that she might be able to quit abusing alcohol. I told her that God would help her only if she was willing to put some personal effort into it. I suggested that she associate with new people who respect sobriety, that she surround herself with a loving, nurturing group of supportive friends, that she take seriously her primary counselor at Alcoholics Anonymous, and then that she pray for all she was worth.

Weeping Willow was a multiple-problem person. Clearly she had at least an initial understanding of each of the three interrelated points I had made. But whether she would remember and recall them, let alone act on any of them, was very unlikely. Yet a conversation we had a week later, although maddening, was most encouraging.

"Hi, Father Mark! As you can see, I'm drunk again. Have you been praying for me?" asked Weeping Willow, slurred and slow of tongue.

"Yes, I have been, Weeping Willow," I was able to answer honestly.

"Then how come God don't stop my drinking?"

"As I told you a few nights ago, God doesn't usually make a person quit doing what she really wants to do. God will give you the power to live a life more pleasing to him, but if you don't do anything for yourself, he won't do anything for you either." Because Weeping Willow was drunk, this was one of those rare times when I felt I was throwing pearls before swine.

Weeping Willow asked more questions about what to do and how to help herself and seemed to have forgotten everything that I had told her previously. Impatiently—and I made it clear by my tone of voice and my body language that I was exasperated—I summarized all that I had said one week earlier. I began to walk away. Weeping Willow tried to keep me there by asking me more questions, to which I tersely replied, "I told you I have no more time for you today," and kept walking.

"God loves me!"

I turned on a dime. "What?"

"God loves me," Weeping Willow repeated with a smile.

"How can you tell?"

Her speech still languid and indistinct, Weeping Willow somehow managed to say most eloquently, "If he didn't, you wouldn't love me and you wouldn't give so much of your time and use so much energy to be mad at me."

I could not believe my ears. The main point in all my dealings with her actually had sunk in. I grinned from ear to ear, backtracked, and gave Weeping Willow an agapic hug.

A Distinguished Name

Showing God's concern for all his creation by loving agapically is infinitely important. But for us to truly demonstrate this love, we must also give respect. When Christians violently push the verbal half of God's Good News in the face of others without respect for who they are, what they are doing, or where they have been, we violate them as human beings.

Bible-thumpers, as I disaffectionately refer to those who evangelize in such a manner, are as disrespectful, if not as violent, as the eleventh-century Crusaders who persecuted Jews for their unbelief. These Crusaders first stripped entire Jewish communities naked, then slaughtered each person who refused baptism. As "Christians," the Crusaders portrayed to the Jews a God of indignity, inhumanity, and outright violence. I, for one, cannot blame the Jews for choosing to die rather than worship such a God.

Many of my parishioners, though not threatened with overt physical violence, are nevertheless undermined by a lack of basic respect. They are often denied the dignity of food, shelter, and clothing—and even ordinary human love. Mr. Alijawan is one of these parishioners.

I called this fifty-two-year-old black man "Mr. Alijawan" to show respect, although Alijawan is actually his first name. I never did know his last name. To ask about last names is too threatening to some of my parishioners, so I leave it up to them whether or not they will tell me theirs.

It was time-consuming and difficult to establish a friendship with Mr. Alijawan. He had had his fill of evangelists long ago. He vividly remembered thirty-three years ago, when at age nineteen he approached a group of street evangelists for either direct assistance or a referral for food for a starving wife and three children. He subjected himself to over an hour of preaching in vain hope of receiving food. When he returned home that same evening, he learned that his baby girl was dead.

At about the time I met him three years ago, Mr. Alijawan had been approached by a pair of traditional evangelists. Not wanting to offend them by simply walking away, he endured their vigorous exhortation for a good half-hour, then finally politely excused himself and turned away. Before he was out of earshot, he heard one of the evangelists say, "Stupid nigger! Probably got nothing else going for him, and he's gonna blow the one last chance we give him, too."

Before I became aware of any of this, I would occasionally enter the Time Without Lounge and see him sitting there, offer my hand to shake, and say, "Ahhhhh, Mr. Alijawan, it is so good to see you once again!" And a smile would uplift his otherwise solemn countenance.

I continue to see Mr. Alijawan an average of twice a month. Every time I greet him he responds with good feeling and some amazement: "You—you—you remember my name. How—how—how is it that you always remember my name?"

"There is really nothing to it," I invariably respond. "It is easy to remember a distinguished name when it belongs to a distinguished-looking gentleman." The broad smile of Mr. Alijawan broadens further, filling his otherwise stolid countenance.

One need not be a psychoanalyst to figure out why Mr. Alijawan is so overwhelmingly pleased and surprised that someone not only remembers his name, but uses it at every encounter. Since his second son died twenty-four years ago, and his eldest son left for another city sixteen years ago, never to be heard from again, and his wife passed away eleven years ago, and the evangelists, who should have been the next best possibility for friendship, failed him—since that time no one had considered him worth the "memorizing" of his name. Mr. Alijawan has seldom, if ever, been shown such respect at any time throughout his life.

It would seem to follow then, that Mr. Alijawan is an extremely lonely man. I have never seen such dire loneliness in another human being. Few human beings are lonely enough to admit it. After I gained his trust, Mr. Alijawan did admit his loneliness to me. He is used to it; that is not to say that he likes it. He has come to believe what people "tell" him—that he is nothing. Because people act in his presence as though he is not there, he feels invisible.

By the grace of God I have done my part to give back to Mr. Alijawan his dignity and humanity through respect. In the New Testament the groups most receptive to the gospel were family and friends. That is because within these groups a person's concerns and convictions are respected and listened to. In summary: We must be good news before we can share the Good News.

Flying Nun of the Eighties

To exhibit God through profane evangelism, to take God outside our temples and bring him to the people, we need more of the foregoing qualities of patience, humility, love, and respect. We also need to exercise the freedom we have in our Lord Jesus Christ. We need to think about and experiment with new ways to portray our God accurately. During the summer of 1987 I experimented by evangelizing in Uptown on roller skates. My doing so has led a considerable number of people to rethink the image of a fossilized God projected by many churches. Many in Uptown have reopened their God file to note that perhaps, like this evangelist, God is real and relevant. Under those circumstances it is worth being known by Uptown's youth as the Flying Nun of the Eighties.

Chapter 5

Witnessing to the In-laws

As important as it is to exhibit God by the qualities we model to others, it is all for nought if we are not also in the right company. We show God's message by whom we are with. This was Jesus' primary message to the Pharisees. Jesus came to save the lost, so he went to the lost to demonstrate that fact. He consistently and quite colorfully showed that God does not sanction the "we-them" mentality. Immanuel means "God with us"—*all* of us.

Knowing God is with us will make us realize that evangelism is bigger than "soul-winning." Suppose that for a day God let you know the final outcome of other people's lives. Let me take a walk with you in your community and see what the prospects for evangelism would be under these circumstances.

Mr. Porter: The Shalom of Christ to Come

"Wow!" I exclaim, looking around. "This is quite the community you live in. Such immaculate and well-kept landscapes.

If their yards are indicative of your neighbors' lives, they really have got it together . . . what?"

"There is Mr. Porter," you say.

Together you and I turn to watch a tall, gray-haired man climb into his Cadillac.

As his car disappears around a bend, I say, "Now look at Mr. Porter's life-to-come. What do you see?"

"Hmmm. Looks like in the end, no matter what, Mr. Porter is going to hell."

"Look more at what happens before the end, though."

"Look at that! Mr. Porter regularly beats his wife. I never knew that! No wonder Mrs. Porter seldom leaves the house and always wears so much make-up. That lousy son-of-a . . . see if I ever talk to that—that—that—that jerk again!"

I smile wryly. "Well, that is one option for dealing, or rather, *not* dealing with Mr. Porter."

"Why should I waste my time with that man?" you ask indignantly. "He's not going to accept Christ as his Savior in the end anyway. He's going to get what he deserves."

"Uh-uh-uh." I shake my finger chidingly. "We all deserve what Mr. Porter is going to get."

"Oops! I forgot."

"Now, then, see what other patterns you can discover in the life of Mr. Porter."

You squint a bit, concentrating hard in order to find the patterns.

"Oh, look! There are a dozen or so rather lengthy stretches of time when Mr. Porter will not abuse his wife."

"Well, yeah, at least not physically. Why do you suppose?"

"Hmmm. Hard tellin'. The several times various church canvassers come knocking to testify concerning Christ will have no effect."

"None at all. So what *does* precede each of the time periods in which Mr. Porter treats his wife a little more humanely?"

"Let's see! The first time he will be in the hospital for seven months. What does that prove?"

"Nothing. Look on."

"Ah, there it is! The second, third, fourth, seventh, eighth, ninth, tenth, and eleventh times are preceded by Mr. Porter's coming into contact with Christians."

"Not all of them are Christians, but most of them are," I observe.

"Oh, I guess the others represent those touched by common grace."

"Exactly! What is it about Mr. Porter's contact with those Christians that make the difference?"

"It's hard to tell. It seems as if the Christians don't do much but keep Mr. Porter company and help him with some odd jobs that he can't do on his own."

"What goes through Mr. Porter's mind during and after the time these Christians spend time with him?"

"The timeline of Mr. Porter's life glows brilliantly at these times in his life. He seems to feel pretty good about life in general right then. But what does that have to do with evangelism per se?"

"Notice God's reaction."

"Oh, wow!" you exclaim. "Those are the only points in the halftime of Mr. Porter's life that are not drenched with the tears of God."

"Why, do you suppose?"

"I have no clue."

"Because those are the times when God, unless he were to intervene supernaturally, is able to most clearly get the Good News to Mr. Porter that he loves him."

"That's evangelism?"

I nod. "Sure, for two reasons. First, whenever we show the world the way God meant things to be, we necessarily move in the direction of the transformation of the world, which will be consummated when Jesus comes back. Mr. Porter's wife will get a foretaste of the new world when, after Mr. Porter experiences God's love, Mrs. Porter tastes, even briefly, of the shalom of Christ to come."

"Yeah, I can see how that works," you respond.

"Anyway, Mr. Porter's life also teaches us that whether or not people will come to our churches, we must go to them. The Great Commission commands us to reach out, and then if there is an opening, to baptize and teach. We aren't commanded to reach out *only if* someone is open to baptism and teaching. That would be a silly command. Except for today, you and I have no way of knowing if people are open to baptism and teaching unless we first reach out to them. Besides, as you can see, it pleases God when we exhibit his love regardless of the outcome. And we cannot show love unless we are willing to be with people regardless of the outcome."

You nod thoughtfully. "I'm beginning to understand. If God waited to love any of us until we were worthy of his love, we'd all be in trouble."

"Well, said." I smile. "Before we continue our walk and meet more of your neighbors, let's sit on this bench while I give you another example and tell you a story from my experiences in Uptown.

"First, the example: Jesus, of course, has all foreknowledge. Suppose he were in Uptown. Surely he would meet two people who were starving to death. If one of them were destined for hell and the other for heaven, would Jesus treat them any differently? Would he say to the first, 'Starving, huh? I've got some more bad news for you. When you are finished starving to death, you are going to hell.' Of course not! Jesus' compassion would extend to both persons, and he would feed both of them. Just as God is with us all, we must be with the people God calls us to be with and in this way testify to God.

"Now, then, a real-life example: One night, as I was walking on Magnolia Street south of Wilson, suddenly about a dozen members of the Gaylord gang went flying by me with baseball bats and bottles and knives. I thought I even saw a gun bulging underneath someone's coat. The Gaylords are a gang of whites who are very open about their hatred for blacks.

"On this particular night these twelve or so Gaylords were trying to catch up to three black men. Chasing them through a vacant lot, one of the Gaylords grabbed at the coat of one of the black men. The black man shook his coat off and ran for all he was worth. All three of them got away.

"Several minutes later, when the excitement had died down, I and a volunteer who was with me on this particular night approached a group of Gaylords who were still in the vacant lot. Roughly ten minutes later, a squad car jumped the curb, came screaming through the lot, and skidded to a halt beside us. The black fellow who had had his coat stolen was with them. The police handcuffed, threatened, and roughed up, not only the Gaylords who were there, but my friend and me as well. The police persuaded the black fellow not to press charges if the Gaylords returned his coat immediately, and so the whole matter was settled in that way.

"My friend and I continued to talk with the Gaylords for quite some time after the incident. Days later, as I continued to spend time with the Gaylords, some of them surprised me with their insight. By their questions they revealed quite clearly that they had gotten the message that was my hope and intention all along. My answers to their questions were 'No, I'm not racist' . . . 'Yes, I think it's a sin to hate anyone' . . . 'Yes, that's why, despite disapproval of your actions, I do not hesitate to befriend you' . . . 'Absolutely! Even though you are "naughty," as you put it, Jesus' love is unconditional and so mine is too.'

"So even who we choose to be with can prove to be a powerful evangelistic message," you say, deep in thought, as we sit silently on the bench for a moment.

Roma: Show, Don't Tell

"Let's keep going," I say, finally, and stand up. "I'm anxious to see a few more life stories before our gift of foreknowledge expires."

You scan the area. "Oh shoot, there doesn't seem to be anyone else out today."

"We don't have to see them to perceive them. Who lives there?"

"Roma."

"Let's look at Roma's lifeline then."

"Good!" Your voice grows cheerful. "Roma's life should have a much happier ending. I know that that woman bends over backward for her church. And her personal life is simply model. Her Sabbath observance is meticulous, and her relations with others are impeccable.

"I see, but it's not all as fine for Roma as it appears."

"What do you mean?"

"Her ending is no different than Mr. Porter's."

"Lord, have mercy! I thought God was a just God. Roma will be religious her whole life long but she will not make it either."

"God is just. Surely you see the core mistake of her life."

"But she will be so close. Couldn't someone have explained to Roma that salvation is not a matter of right ritual or even beliefs, but a humble acceptance of an absolutely free gift in Jesus?"

"Again, it appears that many have and will have tried."

"Is there any hope for Roma?"

"I am afraid we have been allowed to see the bottom line of her life. Of course, when our gift of foreknowledge expires with the setting of the sun, we will no longer remember the future of the people whose lives we scan today. We couldn't possibly live with such knowledge."

"What can I learn from Roma's life that will enable me to be a more effective and relevant witness from now on?"

"Well, in two cases so far today you have seen that wholly verbal evangelism has not cut it. Any clue why?"

"I cannot put my finger on it, but I have a sense that some very crucial piece of the gospel message has been absent from the verbal testimonies I have heard in the lives of both Mr. Porter and Roma so far."

"You are on the right track then. You see, Jesus could have incarnated a human being, gotten in trouble, and been crucified and raised again all in the course of one day. In that same period of time he could have seen to it that faithful disciples would get the Word out about him."

"Don't you think it would have resulted in significantly fewer people finding Jesus believable?"

"Bravo! Exactly my point. Traditionally the church has perceived of evangelism as wholly and exclusively a verbal endeavor; and this, despite the fact that Jesus' primary mode of proclamation—flesh—has convicted and convinced more hearts than all the verbiage accumulated since he was here on earth."

"Aha! In other words, instead of the church and door-to-door Christians *telling* Roma about Jesus, they should have *shown* her Jesus."

"Yes. Generally speaking, you can't truly believe in Jesus until you experience his presence and his relevance in your life."

"I think I understand. Can you give me an example or two just so I can make sure I am clear on this?"

"Sure. Again, I'll draw from my experience as an evangelist in Uptown. It was one of those midwestern January nights when the wind itself is cold enough to freeze you to death. Janice decided that the weather offered a good excuse to take in some 'antifreeze.' Her 'car' called for one-part water, but Janice stubbornly absorbed her 90-proof 'antifreeze' undiluted. On her way home, Janice's 'car' conked out, and she ended up in a snowbank.

"Although she clearly risked freezing to death, nearly all passers-by ignored Janice. The few people who did give any attention turned up their noses. My decision to help Janice wasn't automatic, for it, too, involved great risk. Janice's destination, two blocks away, was a hotel filled with brutal drug dealers. Not only that, but the hotel was on a street with one of the highest crime rates in Chicago. Just a week earlier in that neighborhood, a twenty-two-year-old American Indian woman had been raped, battered, mutilated, and left with a broken neck.

"I finally concluded, all things considered, that Janice's chances of being harmed or freezing to death were far greater than the chance that I might be harmed. So as I struggled to bring Janice to her feet, I breathed a prayer request for guardian angels.

"Having completed my mission with considerable anxiety, I leaned back against the chain-link fence in front of the hotel to catch my breath. Just then a man in his mid-thirties called to me from a window on the eighth floor: 'Hey Rev!' he hollered, 'I wasn't gonna take my wife back if she didn't make it home tonight. But if God cares that much, I guess I should too.'"

You comment, "I suppose you could have preached to this man until you were blue in the face and done no good, but your actions showed him immediately that Christ, through you, was with his wife—and so with him too."

"I'm glad you understand."

You ask another question. "Do you see any one basic evangelistic principle from looking at these people's timelines?"

"Well, I already talked about the need to embody Christ in our lives."

"Yeah, I understand that. I just wondered if there were some good principles to keep in mind so I could do that more effectively."

"A key, I think, is something I mentioned earlier. Namely, we church people have to sabotage the 'we-them' mentality. And there is the 'we-them' mentality even in the case of Roma; otherwise, why would she be working overtime to feel like a 'we'? The key to overcoming this 'we-them' syndrome is to take our favorite image of the church and 'milk' it for all it's worth—take it to its logical extreme. That's the image of the church as family."

"Go on."

"Okay. What is the first word that comes to your mind when I say 'family'?"

"Sibling."

"Good. What else?"

"Relative."

"Good, only took me two tries to get to the word I was aiming for. What does 'relative' mean?"

"To be related," you say in a dry tone.

"Aha! So relatives are related. Would you say that that necessarily implies a relationship?"

"Of course! A relationship is the condition or fact of being related."

"Who are a Christian's brothers and sisters?"

"Okay! I see where you are going with this. If the church's brothers and sisters are supposed to be everyone, and the church is related or relevant only to those who are members, or perhaps to a few others who enter their church building, then the church is largely irrelevant."

"Excellent! Or to put it more succinctly, vacuum evangelism is irrelevant and therefore impractical and ineffective."

"So what is the flip side of that?"

"We must be *with* people in the full sense of the word. Jesus was with us in a way we will never be able to be with others, but we are called to be Christlike in this area also. As I said earlier, who Christians are *with* is a big part of their message about God."

"Can you give me an example of that from your Uptown experience?"

"Sure! Let me tell you about my homeless kids, because this model is particularly relevant to them. In our studies of homeless youth we have found that a minimum of 90 percent of these kids have been physically abused by an adult in their natural family. This is a primary reason for kids running away. To these kids an adult is someone who abuses. They have been taught to distrust all adults, including authority figures. And social workers can't figure out why these kids won't come to their offices for help!

"In the meantime, these kids experience *more* abuse from adults. They have been in and out of the hands of abusive foster parents. They have dealt with the cold and detached and sometimes abusive police. Recently a kid told me, 'The only good cop is a dead cop.' When I asked why he felt this way, he told me that two policemen, who thought he had information they wanted but he wasn't giving up, took him to the lake and beat his face to a pulp. I then recalled seeing the youth's face that way a couple of months earlier and assuming it was the result of gang activity or a drug connection. More recently an adult mentioned that this 'taking to the lake' was a regular activity of some of Uptown's police force. I used to try to modify the kids' awful view of the police. Instead, they have made me see their side. In addition, both male and female youths in prostitution are abused by pedophiles or pimps and 'johns.'

"I cannot blame these kids for not wanting to go to the office of a social worker. I cannot blame them for not wanting to go to any place, including the church, where there are adult authority figures. But here is where the church has a decided advantage. We are the best equipped organization for flexibility. God's work is not confined to buildings and offices. God's willingness to help is not conditional; it doesn't come with strings attached. God's evangelists, including the unordained, have the advantages of confidentiality. God's workers are best equipped to deal with all aspects of one's needs—physical, social, emotional, and spiritual. The church doesn't give detached, cold assistance, but holistic, warm, personal concern. Kids won't come to the church. No big deal—the church can go to the kids. When the church does so, it will find out there are also whole groups of adults who will not 'go to church' for very similar reasons."

"Wow!" you say, "Now I see how just being around certain people as a Christian is evangelism—it's showing God to these kids. So you're the father most of these kids never had, and at the same time you introduce them to the only Father who will ever really matter."

"Yes. Or Mother."

"True."

"You see, then, that in order for the church to be relevant it has to be family to the people around it?"

"Oh yes! I see it clearly now. Look, the sun is going to set in an hour. Can we look at the timeline of at least one more person's life today? This has helped me a lot. I used to feel guilty for feeling that verbal evangelism did more harm than good; now I can see my feelings were right. Evangelism should be much more natural than knocking on doors—and more effective, too."

"I hope you'll let other people know what you learned today."

You nod your head vigorously. "Oh, I will!"

Mike: Surrounded by Christians

You spot a car coming down the street. "Here's Mr. McIntosh's son, Mike, home from work. Can we look at his timeline?"

"Let me take a quick look at it first. I would like to find an example of someone who . . . oh yes, this will do just nicely. God's providence today has even extended to our selection. I was about to say that I would like an example of someone who is actually led to Christ exclusively by the presence of a Christian. Mike's life is a great example of this."

"Whew! I'm glad we're concluding with a timeline that has a happy ending."

"And this is better than I thought. Mike has a life that many will consider nothing short of ideal."

"I guess so! Look at that! He will graduate from both college and law school *summa cum laude*."

"He will start his practice at forty-five thousand a year. He will have a loving and gorgeous wife and three darling children. Vacations, loving family, peace, joy, the whole 'shebang.' "

"God truly does cause it to rain on the just and the unjust alike, doesn't he?"

" 'Unjust' is the word for it, isn't it? Mike won't care what the results of his actions are for others as long as his family's long and happy life is maintained."

"But there seems to be a change in the pattern midway through his career in law. Look there!" You point at the timeline. "Mike's business ethics seem so, uh, well, *Christian*. And look at that! Mike becomes a Christian eleven years after his actions begin to reflect those of a Christian."

"Can you tell why?"

"No. He switches law firms at that point in his life, but I don't see why that would make him act like a Christian."

"The switch in law firms is a definite clue."

"Oh, now I see—he's surrounded by Christians! I didn't even notice that at first because none of them will testify to him about life in Christ, at least verbally."

"They don't need to. They *show* him Christ just by being with him and being what they are—Christlike ones."

"Why do you think they choose Mike to be on their staff?"

"Obviously, because he's a very good lawyer."

"Being a Christian is not a prerequisite to joining this firm?"

"No, just being willing to do some *pro bono* work for the unjustly accused who cannot otherwise afford a good lawyer."

"Ah, I see. Mike's life is lacking in one respect: justice. This Christian law firm, unlike most churches, will welcome Mike into their midst, *not* on condition that he consents to their 'doctrine,' but rather if he *behaves* as if he consents to their doctrine."

"Well said. Do you know many evangelists who are aware of and realize the power of this principle?"

"Not really."

"No, generally evangelists go straight for the heart. Often they get the heart but remove it from a stony body. Hearts do not live long outside the body. It is more effective first to get the body to behave as if it encompasses a heart of flesh. Later the stony heart will be much more easily removed and replaced with a heart of flesh. Only God is truly capable of doing that surgery anyway."

"Just by virtue of who we are with as Christians, then, we are able to exhibit a living God and his relevance and message—even to the point where people accept Jesus Christ as their personal Savior and Lord of their life?"

"Assuming they know that we are motivated as Christians and that they have knowledge of at least the gospel basics, yes. And you'll notice that in Mike's life, too, this exhibition of God was carried out in the context of family."

Witnessing to the In-laws

"You seem to enjoy the Socratic method of teaching, Mark. What one question would you like to leave me with?"

"I judge a question as helpful by whether I've struggled with the question myself. So let me preface my question with the story of the struggle that brought on the question.

"I went to court with Norma, a twenty-six-year-old woman who is constantly beaten by her husband. She had finally taken my advice, gotten a restraining order for protection, and was pressing charges against him. I have counseled both parties in this relationship. Both, of course, have contributed to the breakdown of the relationship. But I still encouraged Norma to press charges because I had diagnosed her husband as antisocial and sociopathic.

"I have been in a lot of courtrooms for a lot of different cases, but this scene was the most depressing of all. It was a court for domestic violence. Sitting in this courtroom I felt a sense of the imminence of the coming again of Jesus as never before. There was a case brought by a son against a father, wives against husbands, a mother against a daughter, brothers against brothers, and so on. Immediately I was reminded of the verses that say in the end times children will turn against their parents, parents against their children, in-laws against in-laws (Luke 12:49–53). But these people in the courtroom, unlike those in Luke, were not divided on account of the Messiah. I could scarcely hold back my tears. Silently I cried out *Maranatha!* And when my eyes were opened and I saw that God saw fit to tarry, I then asked him to help me understand the answer to the question that I now leave with you:

> "How, O God, can the bride of your Son Jesus most effectively minister to her in-laws?"

Chapter 6

Night Crawler

God is profane. God is outside our temples as well as inside. He is in the world, working toward the transformation and redemption of all his creation. I have illustrated how a Christian's appearance and manner can exhibit God's existence among all people and his message and concern for them. I have also shown that we can exhibit God simply through our presence among unbelievers.

In addition to how we go and with whom we go, *where* we go also affects how we exhibit God. Of course, the people we are with will often determine where we go, or vice versa. In the last chapter I talked about my work with whole groups of people such as homeless youth. In that chapter I could also have discussed the group of people in prostitution or those who deal drugs. Instead I have chosen to make an artificial distinction and discuss these people in the context of *where* I go to exhibit God. So rather than talking about being with people in prostitution, I will talk about exhibiting God in a place, namely, "prostitute row."

Going Outside

The single most important place the Christian needs to go in order to exhibit God is outside—outside the church, outside the home, outside the comfortable Christian circle. How will our neighbors know we are Christians? By seeing us enter a church building on Sundays? No, they will know we are Christians by our love. And how can we love people if we are not outside *with them*? If Christians are not seen outside of their churches and concerned for their community and their neighbors, then they are misleading others at best and misrepresenting God at worst. "Insider" Christians portray a God who is interested only in what goes on inside our earthly temples. They portray a God who is desperately trying to salvage a few souls out of a creation over which he no longer has control.

One night as I was making my round on Leland, a young girl, eleven years old, came boldly up to me and said, "Hi, Mark, I'm B-Doll! That's my street name anyway." I had never seen B-Doll before, but she had heard about me when she was "toying" with homelessness and had met some of the hard-core homeless kids. I thought, "Well, if she can be so bold, I guess I can be bold, too."

I asked B-Doll how she knew who I was, whether she was homeless, and if so, for how long. As she was telling me that she had run away just that night and had been gone from home for all of three hours, her mother came along and found her. Her mother screamed at her. She screamed right back: "You f------ whore!" Her mother grabbed her by her long, blond hair and tried to drag her home. B-Doll broke away and swore at her mother some more. Her mother said something about having to get back to the house and a toddler and a baby, and she left.

B-Doll sat down next to an abandoned building, hugged her knees, and began to cry. All her homeless friends whom she longed to be with were standing nearby, but none of them made a move to help her. Maybe they felt that, their own situations seeming so hopeless, that so too was B-Doll's. Or perhaps reaching out to B-

Doll in her pain would reawaken their own pain. So there sat B-Doll and I having a good cry together.

Finally, through her tears B-Doll asked, "What am I supposed to do? I don't want to go to those awful state foster-care people; they're worse than my mother. But I can't go home; I know my mother will beat me." I asked B-Doll if it would be helpful for me to go home with her, in my collar and all, and see if I could calm Mom down and enable them to talk calmly with each other.

B-Doll smiled and stood up, inviting me to go with her. When we reached the apartment, her mother apologized for the messy place, but was very cordial and invited me to enter and sit down. I explained that I did not want to be nosey, but could not avoid seeing both mother and daughter's frustration in trying to deal with each other outside. Mom apologized, but still made excuses for herself at the expense of her daughter. Naturally, B-Doll got defensive and countered by implicating her mother. I said, "I'm not qualified in counseling, but may I refer you to someone who will help you sort through your problems with each other?"

After I made arrangements for counseling that evening, I hung around a while longer to see if we could have a civilized conversation together and to calm both mother and daughter down before the counseling session. Before I left, B-Doll expressed pleasant surprise that I was an "outside" minister. She recalled that a Vacation Bible School teacher had once told her, "God is with you wherever you go and cares about you and watches over you." B-Doll concluded, "Now I know what she meant."

Barring No Place

To many Christians, bars represent the antithesis of the church. What they don't realize is that by deciding not to set foot in a bar they make it easier for the unbeliever to reach a similar resolve—not to set foot in a church. What these Christians don't realize is that bars are excellent places for them to exhibit God's presence in every aspect of life. I have seen more people come to a saving faith in Jesus Christ in bars than anywhere else. And I emphasize that these barroom conversions were not drunken commitments. The conversions of which I speak were all sober commitments made only after serious and relatively long-term shepherding into discipleship.

It seems that bars fill a serious human need. Our fragmented, mobile, anonymous society thirsts for fellowship, and so bars very ably quench more than one kind of thirst.

I firmly believe that the church is the only other neighborhood organization that is in a position to compete with the bar. Or what's better—rather than competing with it, the church should take advantage of the bar. Let the bar owners foot the utility costs and provide the refreshments. Going to the bar will illustrate that God is truly sovereign in all areas of life. Unlike so many Christians, God does not stop at the tavern door.

Because God is present in bars also, I have had my greatest evangelistic successes there. Often people who frequent bars think they have their place and God has *his* place—in a church, not a bar. This is why so many people get angry when they see a minister in a bar. They think God has failed them, so they have given up on God and no longer want anything to do with him. So what right, they ask angrily, does this minister have to bring God back into their lives?

That was just the way Loretta viewed things. I have known Loretta ever since I began ministry in Uptown. Initially Loretta made great strides toward faith in Jesus and discipleship. Within six months, however, Loretta experienced the brutal murder of a fiancé and a close friend. A third friend was viciously stabbed with a knife. Loretta herself was the brunt of a number of violent acts. And finally, her only daughter was raped.

All these tragedies led Loretta to feel that powers outside the influence of God had jinxed her. She began to drink heavily, and after the fatal shooting of her fiancé, she was close to a mental breakdown. I counseled Loretta for some time, and during these sessions she brought up other incidents from the more distant past involving the violent deaths of friends.

One of these incidents occurred when Loretta was only five.

She and her best friend were swinging in a neighborhood park, and after swinging as high as they could, they would jump from the swing and land in the sand below. Then disaster struck. Once after jumping from the swing, Loretta's friend failed to dodge the wildly swaying wooden seat, and it hit her full force in the forehead. The girl fell, bleeding, into a coma, never to recover.

It was a freak accident, and it could easily have happened to Loretta. Yet Loretta never came to grips with the incident. For thirty-five years she had subconsciously held onto the blame, and periodically it came back to "haunt" her. As others around her began to die or get hurt, in incidents that were even more clearly not her fault, she continued to pile guilt upon guilt on herself.

Feeling that nothing could relieve her of her guilt, Loretta decided to try to exorcise her guilt feeling through drinking. But the alcohol only deepened her mental anguish. Loretta became chronically absent-minded and suicidal. Things got so bad that at one point, while in a trancelike state, she set her apartment on fire to punish herself as if in hell.

Nothing I told Loretta seemed to penetrate her despair. So I listened to her at length with all the professional listening skills I could muster. This interaction could only have taken place in a bar because, except for her apartment, the bar was the only place she could be found. At this point she still felt no absolution. So I took what I could get, trying to help her cope with "her" responsibility for the tragedies that had befallen her friends.

Loretta began to stabilize mentally and had been improving when another boyfriend was brutally knifed and nearly killed in her presence. To make matters worse—in Loretta's mind—the attack had been intended for her. Her boyfriend had thrown himself into harm's way to save her life.

After that, Loretta really went off the deep end. The next time I saw her, she was in the Time Without Lounge. She said, sadly and drunkenly, "I believed you, Mark. I counted on you and your prayers. You let me down." Loretta was in no condition for counseling, and I probably should have held my tongue, but I said anyway, "I know, it is all my fault that your boyfriend got stabbed."

Loretta's reply was predictable: "No, no, it's my fault. I know it's all my fault."

Loretta had obviously regressed, and there was no point in doing or saying any more that night. I asked some friends whom we have in common to keep a close watch on her for the next twenty-four hours so I could come up with a new approach. Finally I decided to try some reality therapy the next time she was sober and I was with her. That happened to be the following day at about the same time.

I entered the bar, sat down, ordered a Coke, and asked Loretta how she was feeling. I could have guessed her answer. "Plan B is now or never," I told myself. Then I said, "Loretta, I need to say some things to you that I believe you will find helpful, though painful. All I need are two uninterrupted minutes of your undivided attention. Loretta skeptically consented.

We moved to a corner of the bar, and I began to try to exorcise her guilt. "Loretta, you are *not* a jinx," I began. "There has not been one death of one friend of yours your whole life long for which you are responsible. Clearly, the death of your childhood friend was an accident. As for all the others, it is not at all, by any stretch of the imagination, *who* you are that has caused the death of so many of your loved ones, but rather, *where* you are. Let's face it, woman, you live and work in a very violent neighborhood. The police records themselves show this to be one of the most crime-ridden neighborhoods in Chicago.

"I apologize for not saying this sooner, and what I am about to say is brutally honest, but I have to say it because I love you, and I think it will help you to see reality a little more accurately for what it is. You not only live in a violent neighborhood, but for some reason you tend to hang around a lot of 'looney tunes,' further multiplying the odds that someone you fall in love with will be hurt or killed. Those who live and act like fools around here—you've seen it so many times yourself—also die like fools. It is *not* you, Loretta! It's *them!*"

I felt so inadequate. Without the grace of God, my words

would have been worthless, so I asked God to bless my feeble attempt to help. Bless it, he did.

Loretta has been back to her normal self ever since, and this, despite the death of her first grandchild due to Sudden Infant Death Syndrome. Loretta has taken a new job, has moved out of Uptown, and is dating more civilized men. God was exhibited in the place where Loretta most dearly needed him. In fact, God was not merely exhibited in the bars Loretta frequented; he was also present with Loretta there. I thank God that, although many people who frequent bars will never darken the door of a church, he will leave the ninety-nine and enlighten the one sitting at a booth in a bar. And if the bar is good enough for God, it is good enough for me.

The Gameroom Rev

Besides bars, gamerooms are also good places for Christians to exhibit God powerfully. People still believe that God is an ogre who hates to see anyone having fun. Almost daily young people ask me what business a minister has in a gameroom. "The gameroom," I invariably tell them, "is where I feel particularly close to God."

"Huh?"

"Seriously. There are always a lot of children in the gameroom. We are all the children of God. And when we learn these games, just as when we begin to learn about God, we fight them—and we fight God. But when we understand the game, and when we begin to understand God, we can stop fighting and start enjoying ourselves—and start scoring big."

"But a lot of us are addicted to these machines. Do you think that's good?"

"No, but in this respect, too, these games are very similar to the God Game of life. God allows us the freedom to make mistakes. Besides getting addicted to games, we can also make the mistake of becoming obsessed with our own desires rather than enjoying God's creation in honor of him."

"I see. It's like living to eat rather than eating to live."

"Yes, almost an exact analogy."

"Ya know, a lot of kids who have seen you, but who have never talked to you, call you 'the Gameroom Rev.' When you get a high score on one of these games and you get to punch in your initials, you always put 'R.E.V.' in, don't you?"

"Yeah. Is that how I got the nickname 'The Gameroom Rev'?"

"Yeah, at least I think so. You aren't offended by that?"

"Should I be?"

"Well, I guess according to what you said, it's probably a great name. At least for me you make God sound so, well, so real and fun."

Someone Cares

If the Christian's presence in a gameroom exhibits a God who wants us to enjoy life, then the Christian's presence on skid-, pimp-, prostitute-, dealer-, or user-row exhibits a God who wants to be the fun for which the people on these rows have found grossly inadequate substitutes. I do not mean to imply that these people are literally having fun. Few if any of them actually enjoy their work. And "work" here is a key word. The reasons for these various groups of people being on these rows are manifold. The bottom line in each case, however, is that it is an economic issue.

Take people in prostitution, for example. Nearly all of them were physically abused, and most of these sexually abused, before they turned to prostitution to make money. From the beginning they have been given the message that, apart from their bodies, they are worth*less*. Those who buy their bodies reinforce that demonic message. People in prostitution have been taught a pattern of self-abuse. They believe that in abusing themselves they can both please society and survive. So I will be forever puzzled when politicians address the need to "clean up prostitution" and then proceed to hassle its victims—the people in prostitution themselves. *They* are not the dirt that needs sweeping.

The fun for these various row people that God has in mind is the fun, the joy, the delight of discovering one's loveliness. There are none quite so lovely as those who are loved—unconditionally, agapically. Such love wields the power to break the chains of enslavement. Before I began my evangelistic work in Uptown I would never have believed that I merely had to be seen and known as a Christian on these various rows for God to deliver his message of love and caring to their inhabitants. That such is the case, however, is no longer disputable.

Two recent incidents have verified for me the power of profane evangelism. From the start of my Uptown ministry I knew a certain skid-row woman who always seemed void of any spark in her life. She moved very slowly and rarely, if ever, spoke. Nor did I speak to her because, quite frankly, I was afraid of my helplessness before her moribund existence. But after a time, for reasons of which I was wholly unaware, her body and her voice began to bounce with a new vitality. One day, as I was wondering about her new behavior, she approached me and declared, "I've never spoken with you before, but I want you to know that before you started coming around, I was suicidal. Now I know"—she continued her declaration with an index finger pointed upward—"Someone cares."

In the second incident, too, someone I had never talked with told me that merely by my presence in profane places, merely by my exhibition of God, he was able to perceive God and receive God's Good News. Coming out of a bar on Wilson Street, a man declared, "Father, when I see you in a neighborhood like this, taking the same risks that we do and really caring about us, then I know that God still lives and still cares." And this was a man heavily involved in both drug dealing and drug abuse on "his" row.

Night Crawler

Christians can go almost anywhere to exhibit God, but I believe bars the best place. It was in a bar called Shannon's "Holler" Heaven that I met Shannon and her fiancé, J.P. In the summer of '87, these two asked me to marry them. J.P. expressed concern about this to me one night. He had been married twice previously, but he really loved Shannon and wanted badly for this marriage to work. He was quite uncomfortable coming to me because "I believe in God an'at, but I haven't done gone to a church since I was a kid. Ken ya help me still?" We set up a schedule for premarital counseling.

Then I got married myself and took a couple of weeks off. The day we returned from our honeymoon, I got a call. "Mark," the woman said, "you don't know me but I am the sister-in-law of J.P. He has been shot and killed, and we were just going to have the funeral directors do a memorial service. But then I found your [calling] card in J.P.'s personal belongings. I asked Shannon about you, and she told me that you and J.P. were friends and that she was sure J.P. would have wanted you to do the service, and that is all we want. We want to do things the way J.P. would have wanted them done."

J.P. had three brothers and two sisters. His brothers hung out in Uptown as he had done and were also quite often at Shannon's "Holler" Heaven. He and his brothers were all but rejected by their mother; they were illiterate, had a lower-class mentality, and were at a subsistence level of living. The mother and the two daughters, on the other hand, lived an upper-middle-class lifestyle in Florida. Whenever someone entered the funeral parlor and wished to pay last respects to the body of J.P., his mother would invariably introduce her son in a way that reflected her embarrassment over him. She would say, "We have two pictures of J.P. up by his casket. When J.P. was good, he was very good, and when J.P. was bad, he was very bad. So we have one picture of each J.P. up there."

Was she in for a shock when I led the memorial service! J.P. had never been known for his serious or tender side, but no one had ever bothered to search for it either. I mentioned that J.P. had told me that he believed in God. (I did not say this to give false assurance that J.P. had made it to heaven; this particular audience would not have made that connection.) I told the audience how J.P. wanted his next marriage to be a good one and how he was scared of letting Shannon down. And I related that J.P. had specifically asked for premarital counseling and that we had scheduled the first session.

When it comes to funerals, I figure that my primary duty is to help people grieve, enabling them to have a good, healthy, all-out cry. I began the memorial message in a soft-spoken and solemn manner, and at just the right moment I screamed, "Why, God! Why, God! Why J.P. in the prime of his life, at thirty years of age?" Folks cried good and hard. But I think the main reason they cried was not because of what I said or how I said it, but because I memorialized a J.P. who someone else felt was worth life, a J.P. whom they never knew, but could have known and should have known. My words made them realize their mistake and the waste to which they contributed.

What an effect my leading of that funeral service had, not only on that family, but on the whole community of Uptown! The aftermath has been incredible. Every time I see two or more of J.P.'s relatives or friends together, the whole service is replayed. Of course, by now their memory of the service is dramatically different from reality. But the message of utmost importance—the message of hope—has always remained intact.

Oh, how they cling to the few threads of hope I was able to put within their grasp on that day! Oh, how their thoughts have begun to ascend and their behaviors change! Oh, how community has been built in ways that community could never before have been found! Up to a half year later, people were thanking me for "doing J.P.'s service"—people who were not even there. Perhaps most telling of all—and it was quite a sight—was when a "high-falutin'" lady from upper-middle-class Florida searched the smelly and dangerous streets and bars of Uptown to find me and thank me for conducting her son's memorial service.

All this was made possible because I followed God's call to profane evangelism, stepping outside the holy temple to enter a bar. I will never forget my first meeting with J.P.; it was in a bar. He caught sight of my clerical collar, recoiled in shock, and said, "Whoa! They let you guys out at night?" In jest I replied, "They'd prefer that we stay on our knees in prayer on the cold, stone floor of our church basement, but I just can't seem to keep myself down at night." Through roaring laughter J.P. said, "We'll just call you 'Night Crawler.'"

Passing God's Bar Exam

In this section, part 2, we have considered three very basic ways in which the Christian is able to exhibit to God's image-bearers his existence, his presence, and his Good News. We have learned that profane evangelism not only makes its workers go outside the temple, but also affects how we go, with whom we go, and where we go. Our appearance and manner change; we reflect God's agapic love in a clerical collar and blue jeans. We begin to identify with the lost—those Jesus came to save. And we make God's presence felt—in the gameroom, on skid row, and especially in the bar.

Wherever your church is located, think about what it would do for your church, and ultimately for God, if a few of the members regularly sipped pop at two or three local bars. Your presence alone may move the bar patrons to ask the important first-step questions: Could it be that God is meaningful wherever we are? Could God have sent these Christians to this bar on my account?

So important is the bar scene for the church in North America today that sometimes I wonder if our reward in heaven will not be partially contingent on whether or not we have carried on ministry at the local bars. Ministering in the bar is one of the greatest ways to exhibit confidence in Jesus' prayer in John 17:15–16 and to fulfill the calling for which that prayer was offered: the calling to be in but not of the world. Will you be able to pass God's bar exam?

Part Three

EXERCISING PROFANE EVANGELISM: Pointing to God's Footprints

"The King will reply, 'I tell you the truth, whatever you did for one of the least of these [siblings] of mine, you did for me.'"
—Matthew 25:40

Part Three

EXERCISING PROFANE
EVANGELISM: Pointing to
God's Footprints

Author's Note

In the three chapters that follow, I want to illustrate, not only that God exists outside our temples, not only that we should exhibit God through profane evangelism in "unholy places," but also that our message of Good News is even more powerful when we *exercise* that profaneness. By this I mean being Christlike in our actions as we work toward fulfilling Christ's *shalom* in our world.

To know how to exercise profane evangelism, the Christian must first realize the importance of understanding what part of the Good News a parishioner most needs to see. For example, for me to exercise God's love on behalf of one of my parishioners, I need to know that in the past, love for her was always contingent on her actions. To exercise the Good News of unconditional love to her I must first know how she defines "love," then act out God's definition of love in ways that will most clearly convey God's message. Sometimes this process of exercising love is as long and arduous as a marathon run.

For readers to get a sense of this long process, I will tell six stories over the course of the three chapters in part 3; I have divided each of these stories into three parts, or stages. Chapter 7 presents the first part of each story and describes each parishioner's past and the part of the Good News I decided that he or she needed to see. Chapter 8 offers the second stage and describes how I exercised profane evangelism on their behalf. Chapter 9, presenting the third stage, illustrates the power of profane evangelism by describing the changes in the parishioners' lives once they accepted God's Good News.

For the sake of clarity I will label the first third of the six stories in chapter 7 this way: 1^1, 2^1, 3^1, etc.; the second portion in chapter 8: 1^2, 2^2, 3^2, etc.; and the final third of the stories in chapter 9: 1^3, 2^3, 3^3, etc. Thus, rather than reading the chapters in sequence, readers may choose to complete one story before beginning the next.

What's in a Name?

There is really not much to a name, I think. My name is Mark. What does that tell you? That my name is Mark tells you that I am probably a person and probably a male, but that is all. My last name is Van Houten. What does that tell you? It probably reveals very little, and it may even confuse my identity. After all, you might think I am from Holland, when actually I am a third-generation American. Great confusion might ensue were we ever to meet. Because my surname is Van Houten, you might *dink dat ik kan Nederlands goed praten*—I mean, you might think that I am able to speak Dutch fluently—when I really do not speak much Dutch at all.

Dutch names are quite interesting. The Dutch did not have last names until they were forced by the French emperor, Napoleon, to add them. The Dutch people rebelled in a passive manner by adopting comical names that indicated where they were from or what they did for a living. "Van Houten" means "from wood." The first person to take this name was probably a carpenter—but I sometimes like to tell people that I am a descendant of Pinocchio. Seriously, there is not much in a name.

This holds true for God's names as well. What God's names are is inconsequential. Exodus 6:2–3 testifies to this contention. In these verses God tells Moses that he had revealed himself to the patriarchs Abraham, Isaac, and Jacob, as *El Shaddai* and not as *Yahweh*. We know for a fact, however, that the patriarchs were aware of the name of God as *Yahweh*. God does not forget details like this. He himself was making the point that the name by which his creatures know him is less than a primary concern.

The stories of the following people reflect that what God's names are is inconsequential. Each of these people knew at least one of God's many names. Yet knowing the names did nothing to make the main burden in their lives either disappear or become more tolerable.

God of Honor: Eileen

1[1] God is a God of honor. In fact, one of his names is "Honor." Eileen knew Honor, but she knew him only intellectually and not experientially. An only child, Eileen had for the most part a normal and happy childhood. She had many friends at home and at school. She enjoyed school and did quite well in her studies. And her parents allowed her the freedom to be a child, not loading her with more responsibilities than she could handle.

Unless we were especially perceptive, we would think Eileen had an ideal upbringing. This is because Eileen became very adept at covering up her hurt, anger, bitterness, and distrust toward others. No matter what she faced, Eileen would put on a Hollywood smile and shake her head in mock agreement, or burst out in laughter to camouflage her pain, or respond ambiguously to change the subject.

You see, throughout Eileen's years at home, her parents were anything but consistent. They indicated that as long as Eileen tried to do her best at whatever she was asked to do, she would be acceptable in their sight. That sounded reasonable to Eileen. She kept her room clean, did her homework completely and well, and worked hard at whatever other responsibilities came her way.

Yet, try as she might, Eileen never did receive the full acceptance of her parents. They promised acceptance under conditions that Eileen kept; but Eileen's parents never bound themselves to their own promises. It is no wonder that Eileen felt hurt, angry, bitter, confused, and distrustful of others.

In her adolescent years Eileen's pain intensified. Her parents continued to expect Eileen to live up to her promises without upholding their end of the family covenant. Even more detrimental to Eileen, however, was the fact that the stipulations themselves continually changed. Every time she achieved what had been the previously agreed-upon goals, she found that the standards had changed. It is difficult to play a game, let alone win it, when the rules continually change mid-course. Eileen was supposed to get at least *B*'s in school. But when she came home with *B*'s, she was told she could have and therefore should have gotten *A*'s. Eileen was told she could go on dates on the weekends as long as she was home by midnight. She would come home at midnight expecting all to be well, and her parents would tell her she should have been home earlier. It is no wonder Eileen developed a hurt, bitter, and distrustful disposition toward *all* others.

There was no assurance waiting in the wings for Eileen. How could there be? The parents' manipulation of Eileen reaped systematic frustration. Like a carrot dangled from a stick in front of a horse, the prize of parental acceptance was forever just out of Eileen's reach.

Eventually Eileen gave up altogether her attempts to please her parents, since she had no assurance that she would ever be able to please her parents and be accepted. Her parents methodically taught her that she could trust no one. And Eileen fought back with all her armor of gestures intact, smiling and shaking her head in mock agreement, laughing to hide her pain and distrust, or responding ambiguously to change the topic and hide her true self, which she had been taught was unacceptable.

God of Justice: Orlando

2[1] Besides being a God of honor, God is also a God of justice. One of God's names is "the Just One." Ironically, however, this has to be the name of God that suffers the most injustice. The church is always harping about injustice. "Injustice!" shout the churches in the suburbs of Los Angeles, "there are people literally starving to death in Ethiopia!" "Injustice!" rises up the cry from the churches in Chicago's suburbs, "there is apartheid in South Africa!" "Injustice!" shriek the churches in the suburbs of New York, "there are people trying to survive on $216 per year in Nepal!"

It is extremely difficult for the people of the inner cities to believe that their sisters and brothers in the nearby suburbs are truly in Christ or that they truly care. For many others, it is difficult to believe that God is truly the Just One. They keep hearing this truth, but they are not seeing it. The suburban churches of Los Angeles that shout about starvation in Ethiopia are not feeding their own inner-city neighbors. The suburban churches of Chicago that cry about apartheid *de jure* in South Africa are blind to apartheid *de facto* in their own metropolis. The suburban churches of New York that shriek about the low standard of living in Nepal have members who hire inner-city workers at wages that keep their workers living in apartments worse than any mud huts.

We don't realize that our solely verbal witness damages our suburban neighbors as much as our inner-city sisters and brothers. People everywhere are tuned out to talk. Talk no longer communicates. God as "the Just One" won't mean anything until we exercise more than our mouths on his behalf. To show God's justice, we cannot merely move our mouths inside our temples; we must exercise our bodies in Christian action out in our communities.

In Uptown, blacks continue to suffer injustice as much as they ever have. Many neo-Nazi and Ku Klux Klan members live in Uptown, and they have a cross-burning in a vacant lot at least once a year. Bar and restaurant owners continue to uphold secret quotas for the number of blacks they will allow in their establishments. And blacks continue to take the brunt of police harassment and brutality.

Orlando, aged thirty-two and black, is one of my best friends in Uptown. Several times while I was listening to a group of neo-Nazis explain how to them the Bible justified their hatred of and cruelty toward blacks, Orlando came strolling by. The first time, the neo-Nazis hollered at Orlando, calling him names and saying things to make it clear that they felt he had no right to live.

On another occasion Orlando was approaching the store where I was again listening to the "theology" of the same group of neo-Nazis. Orlando wanted to purchase a gallon of milk. One of the neo-Nazis wondered aloud whether Orlando would wish to be "put out of his misery" so that he would no longer need to worry about finding food. Orlando politely declined the offer and stepped toward the store entrance. A neo-Nazi pulled a knife on him and threatened, "If you go into that store, when you come out again, I will put you out of *my* misery." Humiliated, Orlando went down the street in search of another store.

Several times while I was talking to neo-Nazis, Orlando was seen, verbally harassed, threatened, struck with stones, and even chased. Once he was caught and beaten. He may have been killed had he not slipped out of his coat. As he ran away into the subzero night, the neo-Nazis set his coat on fire. Obviously both Orlando and the neo-Nazis needed to see someone exercising God's justice.

God of Parenting: Duane and Rita

3[1] God is our parent, our nurturer, our father and mother. One of the most important roles of a parent is to provide an atmosphere in which a child is able to be a child. Every child has the right to a safe, secure, nonthreatening environment in which he or she is able to grow into the role of an adult at an age-appropriate pace within a suitable time frame. The toddler dares to explore the house, the kindergartner dares to go to school, the adolescent dares to explore the love of another, only with the knowledge that the parent-child bonds remain strong and sure.

Even when we become adults we remain spiritual children needing assurance that when the world becomes too frightening, we can fall back on God and be certain of his continual love and nurturing. If we will accept it, God's motherliness will always be there for us. As Christ said about his children in Jerusalem who were being oppressed by the world: "O Jerusalem, Jerusalem, you who kill the prophets and stone those sent to you, how often I have longed to gather your children together, as a hen gathers her chicks under her wings, but you were not willing!" (Matt. 23:37).

If we have not experienced the love and nurture of earthly parents, it becomes exceedingly difficult to progress toward the knowledge and acceptance of God's love and nurture. When I work with homeless youth, then, I must first exercise for them God's presence as a parent. Duane and Rita are two homeless youths for whom I could exercise God's parental love.

Sixteen-year-old Duane fits the stereotype of the inner-city tough guy. He "calls the shots" on his particular street, standing erect, arms crossed, his face void of expression. He usually says nothing—he does not have to. He has already shown that he owns the street.

One time Joe, a homeless kid new to that street, was talking to Duane. If this fourteen-year-old was the pendulum, Duane was the fixed point from which Joe swings. Joe trotted back and forth in front of Duane, trying to catch his eye, telling him all about his fights with gangsters and his exploits with women in an effort to convince Duane that he belongs on the street. But Duane remained motionless and speechless. Duane does not play.

In contrast to Duane there was Rita. One night I began my outreach in the Galaxy Gameroom. That night I deliberately ignored the youths around me and got into my game. In a little while a girl, who I later learned was eleven years old, came around staring at my collar. Finally she asked me what a minister was doing in a gameroom. I could tell by this and other questions that she was checking out my credibility.

As soon as I recognized this, I actively worked on gaining her trust. I gave Rita a game token. She returned when it was spent, and I asked her how her game went. Okay, she said, but it could have gone better and she wished she had another chance at it. I told her that if she would take my dollar bill and get me some more tokens, she could have two of them—a simple ploy of exercising trust to gain trust. After spending these two tokens, Rita came by again. Pulling me aside, she said, "We gotta talk."

Rita told me that her mother had kicked her out of the house in her pajamas at 10:00 A.M. My watch said it was then 11:10 P.M. I of course wanted to know how it came to be that she was now fully clothed. Rita said that a nun on her way to Great America noticed her and, hearing her story, took her on a shopping spree. Rita had a few clothes in a bag with her, but she said that the nun spent only fifty dollars on her, and it appeared that most of the other clothes would not fit her. Rita's other stories did not jive either, and I couldn't get at or be sure of the truth. Besides, what mother would kick her daughter out of the house for refusing to do all the dishes every day?

Somehow I needed to exercise God's parental love to both Rita and Duane.

God of Faithfulness: An Alcoholic

4[1] My wife, Rosa, and I frequently attend the worship services at the Roseland Christian Ministries Center on the south side of Chicago. We especially like to attend when God begins to seem other-worldly and far removed. This particular congregation has mastered the art of pointing to the footprints of God around them. For example, they have a time of prayer together especially dedicated to the praise of God. Before they begin their prayers of praise, they openly discuss with each other exactly what they can praise God for. They mention the usual praiseworthy attributes of God, but then go on to identify specific ways in which God has affected their lives.

We all praise God for his providence. We all praise God for his sovereignty. We all praise God for his forgiveness. But the saints at the Roseland Christian Ministries Center praise God for "waking me up this morning," for "holding fast to the throne of my heart when I sought to wrestle control from him," for "inviting me back into his presence after I spit in his face by living like someone who did not know him." It was at the Roseland Christian Ministries Center that I first learned to praise God, not just for his name "Faithful," but for what that name means to me personally.

In my second year of college I allowed myself to get caught up in weekend partying. It started innocently enough. I was a very conscientious and hard-working student, and my friends told me I needed to take a break from studying once in a while. Since there is nothing unbiblical about drinking a little in moderation, I finally agreed to go with my friends and have a beer or two. I confined all my drinking to a beer or two and only on Friday or Saturday nights.

At that time, of course, I did not know that I was an alcoholic. Slowly, subtly, alcohol tightened its grip on me. After one or two beers on a Friday or Saturday night I began to allow myself just one or two more. Soon I was racking up several hours every weekend that are completely lost to memory. I began to drink both Friday and Saturday nights, nursing my disease from bad to worse.

At first, both my friends and I thought my drinking habits were just a phase that most college students go through. But that explanation began to prove false. One morning I had to have my friends help me get my car out of a ditch. How did I get in the ditch? I did not tell my friends this, but I thought I was trying to get from Riverbank to Modesto, California, where my parents live. At the time I was 2,500 miles away from Riverbank in Grand Rapids, Michigan.

Defending my drinking became more difficult all the time. In a span of four months I was arrested twice for drunken driving. My first arrest came when I ran into a road sign. After that I began to make up alcoholic alibis: "What do you mean I have a drinking problem? Just look at my grades. I get all *A*'s and *B*'s in my classes. Me, an alcoholic? Look how well I am doing in school, despite working twenty hours a week."

I continued to abuse alcohol throughout college, and the problem continued in seminary. There a professor and a fellow student confronted me firmly but lovingly about my alcohol problem. Finally, in my second year in seminary I admitted for the first time that I was an alcoholic. I became a very angry person. Since I didn't want to blame myself, I blamed God. I knew intellectually that God is "faithful," but I just could not see or believe that truth. Why of all people did God allow me to be an alcoholic? Where is the faithfulness in that?

God of Protection: LaDonna, Lightfoot, and Other Homeless Youths

5[1] Over the nineteen years that I lived with my parents, my seven rambunctious brothers and I had many brushes with death. Some of us were mechanics, some worked in landscape maintenance, and some worked on dairy farms. Our jobs caused many of our close calls. Most of our nearly fatal accidents, however, resulted from acts of stupidity that earned for us the coveted reputation of "daredevil." Whenever our parents heard about our exploits, they always mentioned the guardian angels that God had working overtime just for the Van Houten family. It was no joke. My parents earnestly believe in God our Guardian and Protector.

Thanks to my parents, I am very aware of God's guarding and protecting work in my life. Knowing his name "Protector," I now act out that name in my evangelistic work. I exercise God's protective power on behalf of many people, but especially for the homeless youth. For these youths, more than anyone else, need protection from themselves, from each other, and from the police. LaDonna, Lightfoot, and other homeless youths needed to see the God of protection.

One night as I was sitting on the steps of one of the single-room-occupancy hotels (SROs) on Leland Avenue, a squad car drove up. An eleven-year-old girl named LaDonna, who did not wish to be written up for violating curfew, came and sat down next to me and said, "I think I will just sit here with my guardian for a while." I had known LaDonna for quite some time. I knew that she went to school only half the time, that she was very bright, that she was advanced to a grade two years ahead of her peers, and that— despite her poor attendance—she was still getting A's. I also knew that LaDonna was just beginning to "toy" with homelessness. LaDonna needed protection from herself.

Homeless youths also need protection from each other, as Lightfoot taught me. Lightfoot was seventeen years old and had been living in an abandoned car for half a year when I met him. He made that car his home for another year before I was able to help him. Dealing with Lightfoot opened my eyes to a number of very crucial barriers to dealing with homeless youths.

Most homeless youths run in packs, and the pack is often the first "family" that the youth has ever had. A sense of belonging is, of course, a basic human need. It is therefore very difficult to lead a youth to understand and believe that more wholesome alternatives to one's "family" are available. Why should, how could, a youth believe this when the substitute family includes a mom and dad, who in the youth's eyes represent pain and suffering?

Even if a youth like Lightfoot does come to understand the dysfunctions and dangers involved in his "street family," peer pressure may inhibit his willingness to receive help—especially from a Christian. On more than one occasion while I talked one-on-one with homeless youths, their homeless peers would yell comments like "Hey, Earl, are you gettin' religion?" or "Forget it, Ted! You're in too deep. There's no way God can clean *your* rags!" Homeless youths like Lightfoot need protection from the peer pressure of other homeless youths.

Other youths need protection from the police. One way I seek to protect my homeless youths is to be around when the police have any dealings with them. Rarely do I have any problems with the regular uniformed police of the 23rd District; I have even written commendations for officers of the 23rd. But from time to time I have difficulties with "the secret police," the plainclothes detectives who work within much wider boundaries. I need to be around when these police deal with the youths, especially if they meet on side roads or in other out-of-the-way and dark places. My presence deters police brutality. The police are entitled to leave the youths alone or arrest them, but they are not entitled to harass them or strike them without cause.

The first time I went to be with youths who were being frisked and questioned by detectives, I was on roller skates. I skated up rather close to the six youths. "What do you want?" one of the officers demanded. I weakly replied, "Nothing, I'm just hanging out." That was the wrong answer—it allowed him to respond, "Then get out of here! This does not concern you." I rolled five yards away and skated in circles, but I offered, at that time, poor protection from the police.

God of Love: Denise

6[1] Of the hundreds of names of God identified in the Bible, the most endearing and enduring is the last in my list. God is Love. All the names and all the meanings of the names of God can be naturally subsumed under his name "Love." Countless volumes have been written on God's love and even on God as Love. Yet God as Love warrants our attention because of a basic and pervasive misunderstanding that continues to surface among Christians. This misunderstanding is not indicated so much in what is written, nor is it to be found in Christians' actions. That we Christians misunderstand God as Love in the fullest sense is discernible in our inaction. And this inaction rises from a selfishness that creates a caricature of love.

God's love is agapic. It is selfless and giving. To do profane evangelism, to show God's presence outside our temples, we need to quit doing evangelism backwards, seeking to *get* rather than seeking to give. We should not be trying to get a hearing or to get commitments or to get people into our churches or to get jewels in our heavenly crowns for getting the Word out. Instead we should be trying to *give* a person what he or she needs most.

Denise, about thirty-two years old, did not have much to do with me for a long time. This was quite understandable; she was into prostitution and drug abuse when I first met her and, due to the notoriety of the evangelists who proceeded me, she figured I would be judgmental and condition my friendship and concern on her getting off drugs and out of prostitution. I did not press the issue. To do so would have done more harm than good. Instead I considered what I could give to Denise and how to give it in a way that would not be threatening to her.

Determining *what* I could give to Denise was much easier than figuring out *how* I could give to her. I sensed that Denise needed someone to talk to, someone just to listen, and wanted to lend her my ear. But when I offered to give my time to Denise in this way, she screamed, "That's all I need, some asshole 'goodie-two-shoes' to hear me out and then take away my last shred of hope!" Denise was lonely and needed companionship, yet her idea of companionship was jaded by the falseness of the companionship that "johns" offered her.

I thank God that I never did think of a way to give Denise my companionship, since it would probably have been disastrous. God showed me that I was trying to give all the right gifts at the wrong time. Denise would eventually accept these gifts freely and gratefully only if I first demonstrated God's unconditional love for her no matter where I met her, what she was involved in, what she thought of me, what she said to me, or what she did to me. Denise was tired of love on other people's terms. If I could figure out a way to love her in God's way, I just knew she would sense that my gifts were not masking self-interest. And I was certain that if she could accept God's love, she would also accept other gifts of God.

Chapter 8

"Church" Is a Verb

In chapter 7 I made the point that what one's name is really does not mean too much. I showed from Exodus 6:2–3 that God himself doesn't care what he is called. To say that one's name does not mean too much, however, is not to understate the importance of what one's name means. The patriarchs knew *of* God as both *El Shaddai* and *Yahweh,* but they knew God himself only as *El Shaddai.* This name means "the most powerful God," or "God Almighty." Exodus 6:4–5 tells that God revealed himself as the most powerful by his deeds of might and mercy on behalf of Abraham, Isaac, and Jacob. But just as the name "Mark" does not tell you that I am Mark the caucasian male, husband, and street minister, neither does *El Shaddai* tell you about God as *Yahweh.*

In Exodus 6:6 God tells Moses that he is going to reveal himself now as *Yahweh,* which means "I am who I am," or "I am the Lord." God commands Moses, "So tell the Israelites that I say to them, 'I am the LORD; . . .'" But God does not then go into some abstract and heady dissertation about the meaning of *Yahweh* or "I am who I am." Rather, he explains what he as *Yahweh* will *do* with and for the Israelites. Exodus 6:6–8 both begins and ends with God declaring, "I am *Yahweh*." Between these two declarations lie seven "I will's" of God: he discloses to Moses seven different actions he will take on behalf of Israel, the sum total of which make up the definition of *Yahweh*. The seven "I will's" disclose that, in addition to being all-powerful, or *El Shaddai*, God is an active presence—a controlling and effective reality.

The best interpreter of the Bible is the Bible itself. The prophet Ezekiel spoke about Exodus 6 in Ezekiel 20:5, saying that God's revelation of his name equaled an oath whereby God committed himself to the Israelites. Then Ezekiel tells us that God wishes to make his name known and respected among all nations (Ezek. 20:9). In other words, as Exodus 6:1 shows, the Pharaoh was like a pawn in God's hands, and the Israelites were not any more important than the Pharaoh unless they worked with God to make his name known and respected. When the Israelites rebelled against God, mocking his name, then God judged them for their disobedience (Ezek. 20:4–38).

We are fortunate today because God is still concerned about his name and has freely chosen to give us a part in making it known and respected on earth. To make God's name known, we must exhibit God. That in itself, however, is not enough. We must also work to gain respect for God's name. Respect for God's name will occur only as we exercise the meanings of God's names outside the church.

What follows is the second part of my six stories, the part illustrating how I (and in one case, a brother of mine) have worked to reveal God not only as a presence, but as an *active* presence outside the church. We Christians must make "church" into a verb, keeping the Scriptures as our reference point, but *acting out* rather than verbalizing the Good News. Just as God reveals his name by his actions, so do we reveal God by our actions. Only when we act out and exercise Honor, Justice, Parenting, Faithfulness, Protection, and Love will we fully and accurately reveal God.

Exercising Honor: Eileen

1[2] When I met Eileen she had been living on her own for six years. Her loneliness must have been hellish, for she just could not be herself and open up to others. She had never experienced being accepted just for who she is, and she had never known someone who set standards for love and acceptance and then honored those standards.

I thought of many things I might say to Eileen, because I knew I was in a good position to help her. After all, I knew the Author of honor himself. If I could just get Eileen to trust me enough to let me introduce her to Honor, I thought, she would begin to recover. There is no one so honorable as God. Surely Eileen would quickly see that God honors the promises, commitments, and covenants that he makes with his image bearers. Surely I could point out thousands of episodes from the history of redemption showing that God is truly a God of honor.

"Eileen," I began, after having known her for about six months, "There is a person who has never, never, never made an agreement and then either refused to honor that agreement or changed the rules of the agreement after it had already been made."

"I'm sure," Eileen responded, "but I don't live in the sixteenth century."

"No, this person I know is alive today," I said, attempting a smile of assurance.

"Really, where does he live?" Eileen asked sarcastically.

"No, he is with us here. Right now," I declared.

"Oh, I get it," Eileen said, visibly irritated. "After six months of making me think we can be friends just for friendship's sake, you're going to lay this God crap on me, is that it?" Eileen had progressed from irritation to outright rage.

"I didn't mean it that way at all," I replied feebly.

"Let me tell you something, *friend*," Eileen railed at me. "My parents believe in God, too, but if that is the kind of people acceptable to God, then he is unacceptable to me."

I recall with horror my inept testimony to Eileen at that time. I nearly became her fatal stumbling-block. She had heard many times and not so long ago from her parents about a God of honor. But her parents had never exercised on their daughter's behalf that which they said God is all about. Eileen did not need to hear these things from me; she needed to *see* from me that God is a God of honor. I needed to exercise the honor of God on her behalf.

"Look, Eileen," I began in a remorseful voice, "I am sorry you misunderstood me. Honestly, I do value your friendship—no matter what."

Eileen looked at me doubtfully. "How do I know that you won't just dump me after you get a second crack at me?"

"Eileen," I said earnestly, "You can tell me right now that you absolutely hate God and never want to hear about him again. I will promise this instant never to mention his name again. Although I will be sad, I will still care about you as much as I ever have."

"Well, that won't be necessary," Eileen said, lightening up. "I don't want you to be sad, but you will understand, won't you, if I am suspicious of you and don't, well, exactly trust you all the time?"

I thank God and Eileen for a second chance. Ever since this nearly disastrous conversation I have been working to show Eileen the God of honor by exercising the honor of God in my life and in my relationship with her. Eileen knows I am a Christian. So when she eventually found out that I knew she was involved in prostitution, she thought my friendship would end. But to reflect the love and honor of God, my friendship grew even stronger. Once Eileen was put in prison. When I came to see her, she said that she was not worthy of my friendship and would not blame me for turning my back on her and never talking to her again. But I had no intention of abandoning her.

Exercising Justice: Orlando

2[2] There I stood, surrounded by neo-Nazis, having just heard their theological justification of racism and now listening to them mock and threaten one of my best friends. In the presence of God and before the face of injustice, I had no choice: if I held my tongue, the stones themselves would have cried out. I yelled to Orlando, "Orlando, you know I am your friend and that I am not a party to this sick and distorted mentality of bigotry. I am neither neo-Nazi nor Klan. The only clan I belong to is the family of God. Please Orlando, do not think that I am with them!"

That was one of the most frightening stands I have had to take for God in my entire life. There I was, in the midst of eleven neo-Nazis, denouncing the beliefs that they hold as dear to their heart as I do my Christian beliefs. As I spoke on behalf of God and Brother Orlando, I simultaneously called on God to demonstrate once again his power over Baal. God did just that. My neo-Nazi and Klan friends were stunned into silence. "How can you dare to stand in our midst and defend a 'nigger'?" one of them finally asked. I admitted that it was a very frightening experience for me, but then declared, "As frightened as I am to know what you do to people you call 'nigger-lovers,' I am far more afraid of what I would face from God if I did not stand up for his justice. I am called to be a servant to all God's children. If I turn my back on Orlando, God's justice demands that he turn his back on me. If you kill me, I will rise again in Christ. If God kills me, my death is eternal."

I continue to circulate among these neo-Nazis and Ku Klux Klanners. My ability to do so I can only explain as a miracle of God. But even more miraculous is the fact that God opened the door for me to minister to both the neo-Nazis and the blacks in Uptown. Orlando was in shock when he heard my testimony to the Klan on that first occasion. The next night we talked at length. Orlando had become so bitter that he had all but given up on God, especially "the God of the Whites." I tried to get Orlando to understand that the way God is represented and the way he wishes to be represented do not always coincide, but he had *heard* all that before.

When a neo-Nazi pulled a knife on Orlando as he was entering a store to buy some milk, I broke off my "theological" discussion with the fascists and escorted Orlando to another store.

"You don't have to do this," Orlando urged.

Giving my standard reply, I said, "I know. If I had to, I would probably rebel and not walk with you."

I asked Orlando, "Why do you take the risk? I mean, why don't you just steer clear of this group when you see them and stay out of their sight?"

Orlando gave his standard reply: "I would rather live one day in freedom than a thousand years on someone else's terms."

On the night that Orlando was beaten and robbed of his coat, I ran after him to see how I could help him. He was so angry that he would not talk to me except to tell me to go away. I was hurt and angry too. How could the name of the Just One be defended before Orlando any more? I felt helpless. I threw both Orlando's situation and God's jealousy for his name before the throne of God. I asked God for the chance to be used in a decisive way in both regards.

Exercising Parenthood: Duane and Rita

3[2] Duane had tolerated my presence for some time, but that is not to say he would talk to me more than he did with anyone else. I knew Duane had to be "cool" and in control because of his homelessness; but there was another reason for his "cool hand" that I discovered one day only by accident.

On that day Duane's older brother, Rodney, was throwing the football around. Whoever caught it had to hang on for dear life while everyone else jumped him to wrest the ball away. It came down to just Duane and me being left, and I decided to play the game with Duane to see if he would play it with me. I am stronger and heavier than Duane, so when he ran at me full speed to tackle me, he bounced off me and fell to the ground. After regaining his composure and overcoming his shock that the minister was no wimp, he repeatedly attempted to swipe the football from me to no avail.

It was my turn to be surprised. Each time Duane attempted to take the ball from me, he did so with the laughter and sheer enjoyment of a sixteen-year-old. He was having a great time. I had never before seen Duane act his age, let alone do so unself-consciously,

What was going on? Duane had seldom, if ever, been invited

and encouraged to act his age. He was virtually born with adult responsibilities, expected to be self-sufficient, and forced to protect and defend himself in the cold, nasty city. He had never had the chance to interact as a child to an adult in such a carefree manner. With me, an adult, around, Duane was momentarily able to depend on my nurture and love and could briefly recapture some of the childhood that had escaped him. In our evangelistic effort to exercise the parental nature of God we need to help some people become like little children in the earthly sense before they will be able to become like little children in the spiritual sense.

With regard to Rita, I decided to concentrate, not on what I did not know and could not be sure of, but on what I did know. What I did know is that it was 11:30 P.M., an eleven-year-old was by herself in a dangerous community, she was either kicked out or had run away from home, she was unwilling to go home, and either neglect or abuse was involved. Ultimately I was able to get Rita admitted to a home for sexually abused children where the staff followed up with the police and parent the next day.

I later learned that Rita had no father and that her mother worked twelve-to-fourteen hours a day. Rita was for all intents and purposes parentless. She wished to be a child (and not do all the dishes every day), so she ran away to find parents. The story of the nun was a product of Rita's imagination, providing a mother figure who did not work all the time, but even took time to go to Great America. The nun was a mother who had time to wait on Rita, even to the point of looking after her needs and taking her shopping.

After creating a caring, nurturing mother-nun, what better stroke of providence could Rita have had than to discover a "father" in a gameroom? I represented her long-lost father—and, oh, what a father! This one even played video games. I had to be the father who had been absent from Rita's life. Rita may have been delighted. I was crushed, for it seemed I was not such a great builder of trust among youth after all. What I did for Rita she had expected. After all, I was "merely" her father!

Exercising Faithfulness: An Alcoholic

4[2] Although I defended my abuse of alcohol throughout college and through two years of seminary, I did feel guilt. The power of alcohol over my life allowed me to feel worthless, pitiful, and even remorseful, but it refused to allow me to translate my guilt feelings into true repentance and a changed life. I continually manipulated family and friends into thinking that I was repentant and ready to straighten out my act this time. It was of utmost importance that they continue to believe in me. Each time I knew someone dear to me would find out, I immediately confessed my sins to the person to persuade him or her that I really was sorry and would no doubt do better. As soon as I was assured of that person's steadfast love, I would sneak out to drink again.

God used many people to exercise his faithfulness on my behalf. Throughout my enslavement to alcohol God used many people to point to his footprints outside the church and alongside of me. But I did not see many of those footprints during my years of alcohol abuse. Only after I had finally shut the back door of my life that I had kept open for alcohol abuse was I finally able to see that "Faithful" was more than a name of God in my life.

How faithful God was to me! There are others who drank twice as often and at least as much as I did, yet they never got caught or suffered any of the consequences that I faced for my alcohol abuse. God's faithfulness to me saw to it that I was caught, and in this way God faithfully disciplined me. This discipline was extremely painful at the time. My embarrassment was unspeakable. The thought of the pain and disappointment that I gave to those who loved me was nearly intolerable.

I'll never forget one incident in particular when God's faithfulness shone through in the Dark Ages of my life. One of my older brothers, Andy, had given me a thousand dollars in my freshman year of college to help me through. In my sophomore year I as much as threw away two thousand in court fines and car repairs for accidents stemming from drunken driving. Shortly before my first accident and court fine, Andy had called to see how I was making out financially. I had no idea at the time how I was going to pay for all my second year of college. Andy said he would put another thousand dollars in the mail.

I was so happy about my brother's good-heartedness that I just had to go out and celebrate with some friends. As had become my pattern, I didn't stop celebrating when my friends did. That was the night I ran into a road sign and got thrown into jail. On returning to my dorm I felt as low as low can get. I thought that the only worse thing I could do would be to accept Andy's financial help for college after I had just thrown away at least a thousand.

It took all the courage I could muster to make that phone call to Andy. Singing "such a worm as I" from a church hymnal is one thing; not only to mean it, but to prove it to someone else is quite another. I told Andy everything, not omitting a single detail. When I finished presenting the evidence against myself, I had only my self-imposed sentence to declare.

"So, Andy," I said, choking the words out through my tears, "You shouldn't send the money to such a bad boy."

Andy replied simply and sincerely, "My gift does not depend on your being a good boy."

A thousand times greater than the money is the gift Andy gave me by pointing out the footprints of God's faithfulness in my life. Since then, I have never been able to sing the hymn "Great Is Thy Faithfulness" with dry eyes. Thank you, Andy. Thank you, God.

Exercising Protection: LaDonna, Lightfoot, and Other Homeless Youths

5^2 Since LaDonna had appointed me her momentary guardian, I decided to act the part. I knew that I risked alienating her, but I went ahead and "preached" a little "sermon" to her, my captive audience: "Look around you. What do you see? There is a thirteen-year-old hooked on 'talley' [glue sniffing]; there's a fifteen-year-old who has dropped out of school and is forced to make a living by renting out her body; there's a twenty-two-year-old, and there's a twenty-seven-year-old, and there's a thirty-two-year-old, and there's a guy in his forties and a woman in her fifties, and there's a man in his sixties, and they are all so drunk or high they don't know where they are or what they are doing. They are all clearly unhappy, and you see it all every day. Is that all you want out of life?"

"I'm not out here that much . . ." LaDonna began defensively.

"That's not what I said," I replied. "What the farmers are harvesting this fall all depends on what they put in the ground last spring. What you put in here now"—I said while tapping the side of her head—"will determine what you get out of there when you are twelve, thirteen, sixteen, eighteen, twenty-one, thirty-one, and the whole rest of your life."

As we talked on, I prayed that God would help me to protect LaDonna from herself.

Lightfoot, by contrast, needed protection from his peers. I knew the strength of peer pressure for youths with homes and families, but it took me a long time to see that peer pressure among homeless youths is just as strong, if not stronger.

To counter this peer pressure I experimented in two ways. First, I experimented with my image, working hard to accept youths nonjudgmentally so as to focus their attention on my presence primarily as a helping person and only secondarily as someone concerned with religion. (Call it pre-evangelism, if you will.) In this way I could continue to minister to the youths while reducing the risk of their friends mocking them because of their associating with me.

Second, I used the best bait for adolescents: food. I lured them away from their peers and into private conversations by offering them a meal in a restaurant, off the streets, away from their friends. Using this strategy, I was finally able to provide some protection for Lightfoot from his peers. I fed him the first time with no strings attached and in a setting of general conversation. But I also set the stage by offering to buy him a meal "next week Thursday." That Thursday was the first time any of these teenagers ever kept an appointment with me, and that despite the fact that I attached some strings to this second meal: before we met to eat, Lightfoot had to talk to someone able to set him up in a transitional living program.

Homeless youths unfortunately also need protection from police. I had failed to give adequate protection the first time, so the next time I saw detectives frisking and questioning youths, it was particularly important that I give a "correct" answer and be able to hang around.

One night three youths were being questioned in the middle of a dark street where they were especially vulnerable to police harassment and abuse. I rolled up to the youths again and encountered the same two officers that had run me off earlier. Again one of the officers asked, in even harsher tones than before, "Hey, you on the roller skates! What do you want?" This time I was ready. As calmly and as confidently as I could, given my pounding heart, I replied, "I am speaking with *my* parishioners here."

The officer did not say a word, but his face turned crimson and he looked as though he were about to explode. However, I turned from him and spoke as unequivocally as possible to my three young parishioners, two of whom were fourteen and one of whom was fifteen. I felt that my show of self-confidence would calm their fears. The boys knew exactly why I was with them. Out of earshot of the detectives, one of them told me that he had seen the police beat up kids in dark places like this street three times. All three of the boys thanked me for my protection. And I thanked God for the chance to exercise his protecting presence in their midst.

Exercising Love: Denise

6² My excitement over figuring out that Denise's greatest need was to know God's unconditional love was premature. For how do we exercise unconditional love to someone who is a master at finding hidden motives whether they are there or not? At a complete loss, I confessed my blindness before God and begged him to teach me even more about his divine love. I wanted badly for God to use me to show Denise his unconditional love.

As I prayed, saying to God, "Please use me to bring Denise into a saving knowledge of you as Love," God answered, showing me how to exercise his love on Denise's behalf. First, he reminded me of my own redefinition of evangelism. I had prayed that I might bring Denise into a saving *knowledge*. Dispensing knowledge about God is not evangelism; knowledge of God is as meaningless as knowing what his names are.

Successful evangelism occurs when we help someone *understand* what we tell them about God. Understanding does not automatically make that person a Christian, however. Rather, understanding combined with knowledge helps a person to decide *responsibly* what his or her relationship to God will be. Denise probably knew as much about God as I do. She knew full well that God is love. But her understanding was warped by the "love" she received for a living. She could receive knowledge through words, but she could gain understanding only through experience. Thus, to witness effectively to Denise I had to exercise God's love on her behalf. I had to put the love of God into action.

I had never mentioned Denise's prostitution to her. I thought she might be under the illusion that somehow I did not know how she supported herself. Neither did I mention the drug tracks on her arms. I feared that if I spoke about these things I might alienate her further, ruining the iota of trust that I had carefully cultivated over the last year-and-a-half. It became clear to me, however, that these were the key parts of her life through which I would be able to help her understand God as Unconditional Love.

I began to give Denise condoms to reduce her risk of contracting AIDS in sexual intercourse and little bottles of bleach for sterilizing needles to reduce the risk of catching AIDS from drug abuse. Since then, Denise has daily sought me out to ask if I have any "little presents" for her. That I would even provide such "presents" so intrigued her that eventually she mustered up the courage to inquire how a "man of the cloth" could "deal in rubbers and bleach."

Chapter 9

The Greatest of These Is Agape

That God revealed his name to Israel shows that he was interested in a relationship with the people. *Yahweh,* as I said earlier, means "I am who I am." This means that God is all that is necessary; he is complete in and of himself and needs nothing and no one. Exodus 6, besides showing God revealing his name, also records some family trees of the Israelites who came out of Egypt (vv. 13–27). It is noteworthy that a number of Aaron's ancestors are listed along with his brother Moses. But while some of Aaron's descendants are also given, none of Moses' are listed. The point is that God does not choose people on the basis of their heredity. Moses' descendants were not chosen to be in special service to God just because they were related to Moses.

God does not care who we know or who our ancestors are. God is wholly other and has no need for any of us. Simply out of his goodness God freely chose to have a personal relationship with us. In the same way, God freely chose to reveal his name, and all that

that name means, to Israel. If God had not done so, Israel would have perished. Instead, he chose to reveal his name and himself to Israel as a covenant-keeping God by delivering them from Egypt.

Like Israel, we have no claims on God in and of ourselves. God needs us no more than he needed the Israelites. And we have no better chance of approaching God than did the Israelites. Who we are and who we know is immaterial when it comes to our salvation. In Matthew 3:9 Jesus said that he does not care if we are descendants of Abraham himself: "I tell you that out of these stones God can raise up children for Abraham." Just like the Israelites, we are at God's mercy. God himself must reveal his name to us and then show us what that name represents.

God has continued to reveal himself more and more fully throughout history. We now know God as triune. We know the Son as Son of God, Jesus, Son of Man, Savior, Immanuel, and Messiah. We know the Holy Spirit as Paraclete, Comforter, Advocate, and Guarantee. In fact, God is still so concerned that his holy name be known, honored, and respected that, even though Israel rejected him, God has not given up. God has not only revealed new names to us and told us what they mean, but has done so through visual aids, in the flesh—through the incarnation, passion, death, resurrection and ascension of his Son Jesus Christ. God's names are important, then, because knowing and understanding them brings us into fellowship with him.

The meaning of all of God's names can be summarized with one word: Love. More accurately, God is *agape,* the giving love. He could be no other kind of love, for God is complete in himself and *needs nothing* from us. Why, then, do many of us exercise erotic love in our evangelistic efforts? The question bears repeating: Why are we nearly always out to get? We try to *get* people to our churches or to *get* commitments or to *get* decisions when we should be out to *give*. When we are out to give to others those things that reflect the meaning of God's name, then God will bless our evangelistic efforts and give us the joy of success that I experienced at the end of each of my six stories. Of all those things that we are able to give others in the name of God, the greatest of these is *agape*.

Results of Honor: Eileen

1[3] Eileen, sitting in her prison cell, told me she was not worthy of my friendship.

"Did I say I would be your friend only if you live morally?" I asked.

"No," Eileen replied solemnly.

"What did I say, Eileen?"

"Just that you would be my friend."

"If you'll let me, I wish to continue to honor my promise, Eileen."

Eileen broke down and cried tears of joy. Finally she asked, "Why are you so good to me?"

"Because if someone hadn't done the same for me, I'd be where you are."

"God truly is a loyal God," Eileen confessed.

"When it comes to the honor of God, baby, you ain't seen nothin' yet."

I continued to exercise the honor of God on behalf of my friend Eileen even when it became difficult. Eileen hung out with all manner of disreputable people, continued in prostitution, and for a time tried every drug available. The most trying aspect of our friendship for me personally was when she began to dishonor our friendship. Under the influence of her new "friends" she rejected me and made fun of me as a minister and as a person. Once when, despite all this, I showed her that I would continue to honor my commitment of friendship to her, Eileen spat on me. But by the grace of God I continued to befriend her.

More than a year later, Eileen came to me again in tears. "Oh, Mark, I've made such a mess of my life. Over two years ago I told you about my awful childhood and how my parents could not be trusted. You have been such a good friend to me ever since and I have been so awful to you. I have done to you what my parents did to me."

"That's some insight," I said. "Sounds like you have been doing some good reflecting."

"I have been, Mark. I feel like such a hypocrite. I've been doing to everyone else exactly what I got mad at my parents for doing to me. I am serious about your help this time. I want to learn to be as loyal and trustworthy a friend as you are."

No number of words could have brought Eileen to this point. She had to see the honor of God lived out and experience it herself. She had to be discipled in the honor of God to break out of the pattern of dishonor that she had learned from her parents.

I had not mentioned the name of God since my nearly fatal attempt at verbal evangelism over two years ago, but at that point I no longer needed to mention God's name. Eileen made the connection between my behavior and what God is like and what he requires. Over time, Eileen came to a conclusion that, again, words alone could never have taught her. One evening, bursting with enthusiasm, Eileen combed the streets of Uptown looking for "her minister" to tell me something.

"Mark, Mark," Eileen summoned me breathlessly. "I've got to tell you what God has laid on my heart."

Between the last time she had come to me in tears and the night of her confession, Eileen had made great strides in learning to open herself to others, even to the point of risking rejection. At times her fears proved legitimate, but she had also learned that, despite the pain she felt, rejection was primarily the other person's problem and loss. Eileen fell back on the comfort of her new knowledge and belief that no matter how many rejected her, there would always be One whose loyalty would be constant and everlasting.

"Mark," Eileen vowed, "no matter what comes of it, it is my Christian responsibility to go back to my parents and honor the commitments I have made to them. Honoring my commitments to them is not contingent on them honoring theirs to me."

Results of Justice: Orlando

2[3] After Orlando had his coat stolen and then rejected my help, I wandered the streets for a few more hours. Just when I was ready to give up and call it a night, I ran into Orlando and two of his friends. The three of them had nowhere to sleep. The shelters had filled up early in the subzero temperatures, and Orlando and his friends were stuck out in the cold and risked freezing to death.

It is standard procedure in Chicago, when all else fails in terms of securing shelter, to call the Department of Human Services (DHS) Homeless Hot Line and explain the predicament. The department then directs a person to go to a police station and explain his or her need. Someone at the police station is then to call the DHS to verify the report and ask DHS personnel to pick up the person and provide shelter. I explained this procedure to Orlando and his friends. It had already been explained to them by a church shelter worker, but a policeman at the station told them that's not how the system works and that they would have to leave.

The case smacked of racism, for I had gone through this procedure with dozens of homeless youths with no problem. I went back to the police station with Orlando and his friends. The desk sergeant was very nervous and dismissed the whole incident as a great misunderstanding. I let it go at that, because a person must choose one's battles wisely. The important thing for that night was to find a warm place for Orlando and his friends to stay.

It did not seem likely, but I prayed as I left the police station that somehow this incident would effectively defend God's name before Orlando and convict him that God is the Just One.

I met Orlando on the streets again a couple of nights later.

"That was some 'tall' tension in the police station the other night, Mark," Orlando stated while giving me the customary three-step handshake of greeting.

"You thought I was too hard on Mr. Sergeant?" I asked Orlando.

"Not really hard on him. Soft, but still firm. How did you know you could get away with that?" Orlando asked.

"That's just the point, Orlando," I responded. "We didn't 'get away' with anything. We were merely laying claim to what rightfully belongs to you and your friends."

"Say what?"

"That's right. Mr. Sergeant wanted us to think he was doing ya'll some big-time favor. I don't 'play dat.' God made brick and mortar, wood and metal, and everything shelter is made of. His justice demands equal access to it all for everyone. Mr. Sergeant's part was merely restoring to you and your 'homies' that which society had unjustly deprived you of in the first place. I wasn't bold or brave or tough or nothin'. God himself was demanding justice on your behalf. How could Mr. Sergeant possibly have done otherwise?"

After we laughed together, Orlando said one of the most bittersweet things I have ever heard. "Mark," he said, "it wasn't that I was just rejecting the God of the whites before you came along. It is that I felt rejected *by* him. I have always believed in his existence and all that the Bible says about him, but when you've been told all your life by the majority of God's followers that you ain't nothin', or even worse than nothin', well, then you just can't help but start believin' after while that, although everything about God is true, it just wasn't meant for those with dark skin. But you've been showin' me somethin' else and I'm startin' to believe that what God wants for whites he really does mean for me to have too."

Results of Parenting: Duane and Rita

3[3] When I discovered that Duane needed to regain his childlikeness, I worked overtime at becoming the parent he had missed out on for so many years. It strikes me as ironic that while "typical" teenagers tend to avoid parents and clam up when they are around, Duane would only open up to me after I became like a father to him. Typical teenagers can afford the luxury of acting as if they are in charge as long as there is a safety net of real control down below. But being in control and taking charge was not a luxury for Duane; it was a necessity.

If Duane had looked his age, he probably would have been discovered by the police and become a ward of the state of Illinois. As long as I was around, Duane did not have to worry, because I acted as his guardian. On a number of occasions I intervened between Duane and the police. Had I not informed the police that he was with me, Duane would have been in violation of curfew, processed at the police station, and forever lost to Mama and Papa Bureaucracy.

Instead, I was able to continue as Duane's parent. It involved a calculated risk, for I had no guarantee that I could help Duane. If something happened to him on the streets, I would have forever felt responsible. Nevertheless, had Duane been taken in and "awarded" parents, the chances are he would have lived with them unhappily to age twenty-one, or he would simply run away again and end up who knows where.

As it is, Duane continues to enjoy childhood while I exercise the parentage of God and help Duane obtain the rights of childhood. We continue to play together, and by asking the right questions Duane has come to view his pleasure in childhood as a gift from God. Duane is still not ready to claim the privileges of a spiritual child of God, but only by my exercising God's earthly parentage is there any hope that Duane will eventually accept God's heavenly parentage. Yet the key obstacle has been removed. Duane has received a glimpse of normal childhood and no longer equates God as a parent with his earthly parents who failed him.

I have not had as much opportunity to work with Rita as with Duane. I have seen her only once since our first meeting. She was on the run again, and we spied each other in the Galaxy Gameroom. She knew that I would have to turn her over to the police, yet she allowed me to find her. Rita made a half-hearted effort to convince me that everything was okay with her, purposely making me probe a while because she enjoyed the parental concern I was giving her.

It took me several hours to act like a parent for Rita, counseling her about her frustrations at home with a single mother who was too busy to let Rita be a child. I helped Rita understand that her mother was in a real bind financially and was as sad as Rita that she could not afford to spend more time and have more fun with her. Rita, a very bright young girl, understood quickly and began crying, vowing to help her mother have some fun too. But that promise wouldn't help; it simply added one more responsibility to her burdensome childhood. Finally, the best I could do under the circumstances was to refer both mother and daughter to a more qualified counselor. Then Rita began to talk about her father.

"You have a father around, Rita?" I asked, expecting to hear her fantasizing again.

"I do," Rita replied excitedly. "I go to the Baptist Sunday school, and the teacher there told me that God is my Father and that whoever looks out for me when I am all alone is someone God has sent to me to be my father for that time. That's why I ran away to see you again."

Results of Faithfulness: An Alcoholic

4[3] During the years that I was involved in alcohol abuse I caused many people dire pain. I grieve to the bottom of my heart for the anguish I have caused them. Every day I plead with God for their forgiveness and for Christ to restore the broken relationships.

For those caught in a sin as I was, I hope my story of God's faithfulness will help them extricate themselves from sin's bondage. I know that if God had not exercised his faithfulness on my behalf, I would have caused even more pain to myself and others. And if no one had shown me God's faithfulness, but had rejected me instead, I most likely would have taken the wide and easy road, finding acceptance in a depraved subculture.

As it is, I have good news to share: God has been faithful. God has never taken away his gift of faith to me. When my world was falling apart all around me, I could easily have been crushed, and I would have been if I had had a strong faith in a weak god. But God gave me enough faith in himself, a strong God.

Throughout the history of redemption God has taken that which was intended for evil and turned it to his good. Satan intended my alcohol abuse to drag me, and those around me, down.

By leading various Christians to exercise his faithfulness on my behalf, God has lifted me out of the depths. He is now using my experience with alcohol abuse to help others break the bonds of addiction and lead them into his fellowship and love.

Once Satan used my presence in bars to bring dishonor to God; now my presence in bars does more than its opposite, exhibiting God's concern for his people no matter where they are. Through me God has worked his redeeming power in many lives, leading many alcoholics to sobriety and a life-changing relationship with Christ.

Because others exercised the faithfulness of God on my behalf, I am now able to do the same for many of Chicago's more than ten thousand homeless children and young people. Faithfully I tend to their manifold needs in the name of God so that they may see a God who can be counted on at all times and in all places. I pray that ultimately they will be able to see a God who lives up to his name: the Faithful One.

Results of Protection: LaDonna, Lightfoot, and Other Homeless Youths

5³ Immediately after my "mini-sermon" and after the police had left the street, LaDonna went straight home, and I have not seen her hanging out on the streets at night since then. But she often summons me from her second-story window when I walk by at night, and I stop to talk.

"Hey, Mark, how are the streets tonight?" LaDonna begins our conversation.

"Oh, nothin' to them, LaDonna."

"Oh, good. Does that mean it is okay for me hang out there?"

"Sure, LaDonna," I say, baiting her, "but don't look to me to sign you out of police curfew problems."

"Why did you sign me out a couple of weeks ago?" LaDonna asked curiously.

"A couple of weeks ago I gave you the benefit of a doubt," I said, my face showing that my doubt had never been all that great.

"I felt that your first brush with the law would only serve to mold you into a hard-core street urchin."

"You were protecting me from the streets?" LaDonna wondered.

"And from yourself."

"Is that what God wants you to do?" LaDonna asked, now baiting me.

"Yes, among other things."

"So then, why wouldn't you protect me again? Wouldn't God get mad at you if you didn't?"

"Not nearly as mad as he would be for spending time with someone who should already know better instead of protecting others who do not know better."

"I'm just playin' with ya, Mark. I'm glad God sent you along that first time to protect me so that there won't be a second time. It's nice to know two people who really care about me."

Unlike LaDonna, Lightfoot didn't know that I was giving him a form of protection. But I knew he needed protection from his peers because he would not ask for help in their presence. Moreover, when he was away from his friends, Lightfoot was as easy to open up as a twist-top pop bottle, as I found when we ate together.

"Why is it that whenever we go out to eat I find it so easy to open up to you, Mark?"

"It's difficult to converse on an empty stomach?" I guessed ruefully.

"That's got to be part of the problem," Lightfoot said, careful not to jeopardize future dining opportunities, "But could it also be that I'm afraid my friends will reject me if I show that I give a damn about some things they don't give a damn about?"

"I didn't realize you had that much capacity and skill for introspection," I commented, genuinely impressed.

"That's just it, Mark. If I don't give a damn about myself, who will? All my friends got false I.D.s so they can sign a lease and stay in that S.R.O. They won't help me, so I'm left out in the cold . . . oh, I didn't mean it the way it sounds. You care about me, or else I

would never learn to care about myself. But it's your job to care . . .
so then why haven't the other church people around here helped
who know my situation? . . . Do they think God only watches over
those who go to their churches? You're convincin' enough to me
that God does some 'tall' lookin' out for *everybody*."

*   *   *

I stayed with the three boys for about ten minutes as a means
of protecting them from further harassment by the police. Then I
told the boys I should move on. I would not have gone so far away
as to make the police comfortable enough to do anything stupid,
but I wanted to talk to another group of kids one-half block away.
But one of the fourteen-year-old boys, his voice quaking with fear,
begged, "Couldn't you please stay?" I stayed with the boys until the
police left.

Before the police stopped the boys, I had seen them discreetly
hide some drugs they had been carrying. I knew that after the police
left, the boys would retrieve their contraband. Sure enough, they
tried everything to get rid of me.

"Okay, Rev," the fifteen-year-old said, "thanks for everything."

"You're welcome," I replied, not moving.

"You're too kind," chimed in the pair of fourteen-year-olds.

"Yes, what can I say?" I cordially agreed.

"Well, I guess you have a lot of other work to do now, right,
Mark?"

"Your time is my time, fellas." I had the three of them
squirming now.

"See ya later, Rev."

"Yep. See ya! 'Stay up.'"

I guess at this point they were just going to leave and figured I
would soon leave too with no one to talk to. They began to walk
away.

"Aren't you fellas forgetting something?" I called after them.

"What?" the astonished trio asked in harmony.

"Why, your drugs, of course!"

Their jaws dropped. "You mean you knew we were guilty the whole time and you still protected us from the police?"

"Yep!"

"Can you do that as a minister?"

"Sure."

"But God doesn't approve of drugs, does he?" spoke up one fourteen-year-old.

"Nope. And neither do I."

"Then why did you protect us?"

"I didn't protect you from being caught for possession of drugs. You got out of that one on your own. I merely protected you from possibly becoming victims of yet another crime—police brutality. God hasn't asked me to point out other people's sins, but he *has* asked me to provide the protection to which everyone is entitled."

"Now that kind of God I can hang with," one youth said.

"What church did you say you are at?" asked a second one.

"I lost your [calling] card. Can I have another one?" asked another.

Results of Love: Denise

6[3] I knew that my strategy to show love to Denise was working when, after I had given her some "presents" for the third time, she said, "I need religion, and you give me rubbers."

I finally had my chance to help Denise understand the nature of God's love. I confidently replied, "Caring has never been at odds with the Christian religion."

"What do you mean?" Denise asked.

"Christians are caring people. Thanks to God, I am a Christian. I care about you. I love you. I would be unspeakably sad and angry if you were to catch AIDS."

"But doesn't God mind?" Denise asked, still incredulous.

"Who do you think taught me how to care, to truly care, to love?" I returned the question.

"Are you saying that God loves *me?*"

"Yes. I don't doubt that at all."

Denise began to cry. We were walking along busy Wilson Street at the time, so I suggested we turn off onto a less-populated side street. Needless to say, I was one uptight evangelist; I didn't understand why Denise was crying. We strolled north on Racine Street, and Denise continued to cry amid my silent wondering. Did Denise misunderstand me? Did she somehow misread our conversation and think that God loved her only if he could use her? Who did I think I was kidding? Rubbers and bleach to lead to God? Impossible! Why wasn't there AIDS while I was in seminary so I could have been informed what to do? I will be declared heretical, defrocked, excommunicated.

Above us, elm trees creaked their disapproval. Around us, sounds snuck out from abandoned apartment buildings. Everything surrounding us seemed bleak and hopeless. As Denise continued to sob, I felt that I had failed her and failed God.

"Mark?" Denise broke the horrible silence twenty minutes later.

"Yes?" I faced Denise squarely, ready to reap my just desserts. But Denise was smiling. Immediately I sensed that I had overreacted, and my spirits rose.

"You really mean it, don't you? God does love me, doesn't he?"

"Yes, Denise, God does love you. But I gotta tell you, God loves you no matter what, even if he does not approve of prostitution and doing drugs. I hope I didn't imply that God approves of what you've been doing by giving you rubbers and bleach, because to think that way is wrong and heretical and maybe even blasphemous against God himself, blessed be his name."

Denise listened to my confession of orthodoxy impatiently and then promptly dismissed it with a wave of her hand. "Everybody knows that, stupid!"

"They do?" I asked, still nervous.

"Of course they do. All I need to know is that if God was here now, and if I refused to quit drugs or prostituting, he would still care enough about me to give me bleach and rubbers. Right?"

Here we go again.

"Well?"

"Uh . . . absolutely," I said half-heartedly and trying to smile.

"Wow! Who will ever believe my testimony? I'm a bleach baby believer, converted by condoms to Christ."

And I didn't even give her a tract.

Pointing to God's Footprints

Knowledge of God's name is not a right. God did not need to reveal his name to us; rather, he freely chose to do so. Knowledge of God's name is a privilege, and it is our privilege to work with him to make his name known. We exercise this privilege by stepping out of our temples and going into our community to give people what they most need, whether that is honor, justice, nurturing, faithfulness, protection, or love. If we are faithful, then when our work on earth is finished, "The King will reply, 'I tell you the truth, whatever you did for one of the least of these [siblings] of mine, you did for me'" (Matt. 25:40). God is outside of our churches and already at work, waiting for us in our communities. Because this is so, much of our work will involve merely pointing to God's footprints.

The Rest of the Story

You see that a person is justified by what he does and not by faith
alone.   —James 2:24

Ancient Chinese legends include many stories of famous judges and
court cases. One such legend tells of a very poor man who lived
above a wealthy aristocrat. While the rich man's diet consisted of the
finest Chinese delicacies, the poor man ate rice for breakfast, lunch,
and dinner. But the poor man was no fool. He scheduled his meals
to coincide with the rich man's in order that the aromas rising from
below would enhance the taste of his own meager meal.

One day the rich man got wind of this situation and with great
fury brought his neighbor to court. He was going to sue his
neighbor for stealing the smell of his food. The sage old judge asked
the poor man if he had any money with him. The poor man cried
out, "My lord, I have but one yuan, and surely that is not enough to
please the plaintiff." The judge calmly replied, "Just allow me to see
your coin for a moment."

Now keep this tale in mind and later in the epilogue I will tell the rest of the story.

For the moment I would like to consider another day in court, so to speak—the experience of the biblical patriarch Abraham. Thinking that Sarah was too old to conceive, Abraham tried to help God fulfill the covenant through his handmaid Hagar. Abraham's faith was not yet fully evident; therefore God tested him again. When Isaac was about twenty-five years old, God asked Abraham to sacrifice his only covenant heir. Abraham set out to honor God's request. But what did this prove?

On the one hand, the apostle Paul said in Romans 4:3 that Abraham was justified by *faith* when he finally came to believe that his offspring would number with the stars in the heavens and the sand on the seashores. Romans 4:3 is a quotation of Genesis 15:6, which says, "Abraham believed the LORD, and he credited it to him as righteousness."

On the other hand, James tells us that Abraham was justified by *works* when God saw that he was truly willing to sacrifice his son Isaac. To substantiate his claim, James cites Genesis 22:2, 9 and explains, "Was not our ancestor Abraham considered righteous for what he did when he offered his son Isaac on the altar?" (James 2:21).

So Paul says that Abraham was justified by faith and James contends that Abraham was justified by works as well. This "problem" is one that unbelievers delight in throwing before the face of Christians. Did not James know about Genesis 15:6? And did not Paul read further than Genesis 15:6 to Genesis 22:2, 9?

The solution to this *apparent* contradiction lies in the recipients of these two letters. Paul was writing to the Romans, who generally emphasized the observance of Mosaic law as a means of salvation. Thus Paul had to stress the point, as he would later also to the churches in Ephesus, "For it is by grace you have been saved, through faith—and this not from yourselves, it is the gift of God— not by works, so that no one can boast" (Eph. 2:8–9).

James addressed a much different group. He wrote to people who were established Christians, Christians who already understood that the means of their salvation was by grace and through faith. However, James knew that faith does not stop at belief; instead, faith goes on to work in us, to complete our sanctification, to make us more Christlike. But the faith of James's readers had stopped at belief, and James knew that their faith must either grow or die.

You can rest assured that Paul, like James, was fully aware of the nature of faith. Paul did know about Genesis 22:2, 9 and referred to it in Romans 4:12. Likewise, James was aware of Genesis 15:6, quoting this text in verse 23 of his second chapter. Simply stated, each man emphasized the Word of God that his readers most needed to hear.

The principle involved here is really quite basic. For example, if a minister had a congregation in which many of the people stressed God's forgiveness to the point where they no longer strived to live an upright and holy life, the minister would not (I hope) preach on 1 John 1:9, which says, "If we confess our sins, he is faithful and just and will forgive us our sins and purify us from all unrighteousness." Rather, he would preach the Word of the Lord as found in Romans 6:1–2: "What shall we say, then? Shall we go on sinning so that grace may increase? By no means! We died to sin; how can we live in it any longer?"

James's readers did not have trouble with faith itself. Their problem lay in their failure to put that faith to work. So James was compelled to remind his readers about the other side of the coin— good works. Good works are the necessary counterpart of faith-works, which is the formula for our salvation.

In the post-apostolic era, the church once again began to preach good works, to the detriment of faith. The Reformers subsequently swung the pendulum in the opposite direction, emphasizing salvation by grace alone. It seems that Christians continually have difficulty keeping faith and Christian work in fruitful tension.

I believe that most North American Christians err by stressing faith at the expense of Christian action. Once again we stand in need of a good Word from our God through James. James asks, "What good is it, my brothers, if a man claims to have faith but has no deeds? Can such faith save him?" (2:14). The answer as found in verse 24 is an unqualified No: "A person is justified by what he does and not by faith alone."

Currently many of us have lost the works aspect of our faith and therefore are dead in the faith. This is indicated by our lethargy in church, by our apathy through the week. Sometimes it is all we can do just to get ourselves to go to church because church is so boring. I tell you the truth, church will only be as uplifting as we are. Praise to God will only be as meaningful as our Christian faith. To have a meaningful faith, our faith must be full of meaning. But how can our faith, our Christianity, be full of meaning if we do not do anything with it?

We can read umpteen books on how to swim, but until we actually get into the water we will never learn. We can know the creeds and the confessions, the catechism, and even the Bible, backward and forward, but until we meet God, the Subject of these documents, we will never really know God or the Christian life.

Where do we meet God? Jesus tells us in Matthew 25 that when we feed the hungry, clothe the naked, give drink to the thirsty, entertain the stranger, and visit the prisoner, "whatever you did for one of the least of these [siblings] you did for me." Where do we meet God? We meet God in individual contemplation and in private devotion, to be sure, but Christianity also demands action. Christian living means working for the advancement of the kingdom of God.

By contrast, in Matthew 25:46 Jesus says that those who do not *live* their faith will "go away to eternal punishment." There we have the hard, cold facts, as plain as our sinful nature. God is a God of love, but he is also a God of justice. If our faith does not produce, if our faith does not bear fruit, then we will lose even the small amount with which we have been entrusted, and we will be condemned.

When the word "evangelism" is mentioned, many of us shudder. The reason for this is, in many cases, because of the bad image we have of evangelists, the image of someone who buttonholes the unwary and demands to know, "Are you a Christian?" or "Are you saved?" or "Do you believe in Jesus Christ as your personal Savior and Lord?" Evangelism would be less threatening and more motivating and enjoyable if only others could become members of Christ's body like those of us who grew up in it—if they could become members of Christ's body almost without knowing it, because they saw Christ personified, his presence exhibited, and his will exercised.

Some of us simply do not have the God-given gift of verbal evangelism. No matter. We have just noted that Jesus himself mentioned service evangelism—taking care of the poor and needy—as kingdom work. Service evangelism is of equal importance with and often more effective than verbal evangelism. In fact, service evangelism is often a prerequisite of verbal evangelism. Which is more important—opening the door to someone's heart, or getting in? A Christian cannot let Christ into another's heart if the door is not open.

Emphasizing service evangelism rather than verbal evangelism renders all excuses invalid. Having learned that profane evangelism demands that all of us use our gifts, we have no excuse to sit idly on our faith. God is calling us out of our churches and into the community to exercise our faith. He is calling us to profane evangelism, a service evangelism that gives to those in need wherever we find them.

Often we use church services as a cast on the church's body. A cast on your arm or leg offers a false sense of strength. You will feel that if the cast is removed, you will be able to run or to swing a baseball bat. But in reality, when a cast is removed from your leg you can barely walk; if a cast is removed from your arm, you can barely wiggle your fingers. Within the cast the muscles may seem strong, but actually they are weak because they have not been exercised for some time.

In the same way, the church can be like a body-cast, giving a false sense of strength and security. Whether consciously or not, many of us think that simply by attending church twice a week, all will be well. But although church is a *special* time of worship to our

God, it should be no more than a concentration of the activity that we do by word and deed all week long. We must exercise our faith day after day after day. We must put our faith to work as regularly as we eat and sleep. Only then can we develop a truly strong Christianity.

Most of us have been given faith, but for many of us it is lying dormant. We are in dire need of reemphasizing the good works that are kept in fruitful tension with our faith. Our faith does not stand still. It can only *pro*gress or *re*gress. A stagnant faith must either grow or die, for "faith without works is dead."

Perhaps one reason why we have lost the works aspect of our faith is that we have prejudged the poor and dispossessed. Maybe because of our Protestant, do-it-alone, hard-work ethic we do not think that the poor and needy deserve God's gifts given through us. The attitude of many is, "So what if there are some who are mentally, economically, socially, physically, and spiritually sick? Only out of such trials and hardships can one succeed. After all, did we not pull ourselves up by our own bootstraps? Did we not succeed on our own, pulling ourselves up the social ladder by our own hard work and individual effort?"

Such an attitude is highly ironic if we stop to consider the reality of our lives. Individualism is one of the most highly valued aspects of the American dream. Yet, within the American dream such individualism does not really exist. Even for the most basic of human needs we depend entirely on others. I, for one, am unable to turn sheep's wool into clothing, or trees into shelter. Many men cannot even turn Bisquick into pancakes. You say that, nonetheless, you will never accept charity, no matter what? Really? Have you so quickly forgotten that salvation itself is a gift?

Or maybe like the rich Chinaman who was too selfish and greedy to share even the smell of his food, we also are too selfish and greedy to give the poor and needy even a scent of God's fragrant and abundant love.

Let's return to our story. The judge took the poor man's coin. Dropping the coin, he asked the wealthy aristocrat if he heard the coin strike the floor. When the rich man said yes, the judge declared the case to be settled because both persons had equal claim: the rich man had now stolen the sound of his poor neighbor's coin hitting the floor.

That's the rest of the Chinese legend. The rest of the story of our faith in Jesus Christ is the work we do to advance the kingdom of Christ. We usually think of revivals as verbal witnessing and emotional testimonies. But the greatest revivals in church history have occurred when Christians simply put their faith to work. So I challenge each reader to find some way to contribute just one hour's worth of work per week in Jesus' name. If half of your congregation *actively* begin to put their faith to work, I guarantee that your church will have a revival.

Let us not make excuses for our inaction. Let us not prejudge those in need by puffing ourselves up in arrogance and exaggerating our own self-sufficiency. Nor let us, like the rich man in the story, hoard our physical and spiritual prosperity for ourselves, for we are all weak and faltering creatures, here today and gone tomorrow. And let us not allow the church, like a body-cast, to give us a false sense of security. But let us get to work, outside our temples, in our communities, so that the faith that we receive by grace may be perfected. "You see, a person is justified by what he does and not by faith alone." Good work is the rest of the story.